D0879131

10 Real SAT®s
Solutions Manual

The College Board: Expanding College Opportunity
The College Board is a national nonprofit membership association whose mission is to prepare, inspire, and connect students to college success and opportunity. Founded in 1900, the association is composed of more than 4,300 schools, colleges, universities, and other educational organizations. Each year, the College Board serves over three million students and their parents, 23,000 high schools, and 3,500 colleges through major programs and services in college admissions, guidance, assessment, financial aid, enrollment, and teaching and learning. Among its best-known programs are the SAT®, the PSAT/NMSQT®, and the Advanced Placement Program® (AP®). The College Board is committed to the principles of excellence and equity, and that commitment is embodied in all of its programs, services, activities, and concerns.

For further information, visit www.collegeboard.com.

Copies of this book (item # 007042) are available by order through College Board Publications, P.O. Box 869010, Plano, TX 75074-0998, (tel.: 800 323-7155), or through your local bookstore. The price is $7.95 per copy. Purchase orders above $25 are accepted.

Editorial inquiries concerning this book should be addressed to The College Board, 45 Columbus Avenue, New York, NY 10023-6992.

Copyright © 2003 by College Entrance Examination Board and Educational Testing Service. All rights reserved. College Board, Advanced Placement Program, AP, SAT, and the acorn logo are registered trademarks of the College Entrance Examination Board. PSAT/NMSQT is a registered trademark of the College Entrance Examination Board and the National Merit Scholarship Corporation. Visit College Board on the Web: www.collegeboard.com.

Contents

Preface

This book is a supplement to the Second and Third Editions of *10 Real SATs*, which contains actual, recently administered SATs. This book contains explanations by the assessment experts who develop the SAT I: Reasoning Test. Explanations are included for all the questions from the Saturday, January 2000 test and the Sunday, May 2000 test.

How to Use This Book

The answers are intended for use after taking the practice tests in *10 Real SATs*. If you do not have a copy of *10 Real SATs*, we recommend that you purchase one and practice at least on the two tests included in this book before looking at the answers and explanations. *10 Real SATs* can be purchased through College Board Publications (800 323-7155), online at www.collegeboard.com, or at your local bookstore.

After you've taken the practice test, you're ready to learn the correct answers. Read the correct answer choice and its explanation before reading the explanation of an incorrect answer; the explanation for the correct choice may include details that are relevant to understanding the incorrect answer choice.

How This Book Is Organized

The *10 Real SATs Solutions Manual* arranges the test sections in the same order in which they appeared when they were administered, with the equating section removed. The equating section includes new test questions for future SATs and helps ensure that your test score is comparable to scores on other SATs—it does not count toward your final score. You should therefore note that there are only six sections in the tests in this book, instead of the seven that are present during the actual test.

The solutions show the actual test question, the correct answer, then an explanation. In most cases, incorrect answers and their explanations (telling you why an answer is incorrect) are also included.

How This Book Can Help You

You're already off to a good start! You have taken an actual, full-length test from *10 Real SATs* to get real practice. This solutions manual will help you understand how an answer was derived, and the relevant concept. Written by the test makers themselves, this accurate information comes directly from the source!

SAT I: Reasoning Test

Saturday, January 2000

Section 1

Each question is followed by the correct answer choice and an explanation for why it is correct. In instances where common errors are likely to occur, questions will also be followed by ONE incorrect answer choice with an explanation for why it is incorrect.

SECTION 1

1. If $4 + y = 7$, what is the value of $4 \times y$?

   (A)   3
   (B)   12
   (C)   28
   (D)   44
   (E)   49

Choice **(B)** is correct. Solve the equation $4 + y = 7$ for y; $y = 3$. Therefore, $4 \times y = 4 \times 3 = 12$.

WORKDAY ABSENCES AT EMPIRE PROCESSING PLANT

Month	1994	1995
January	18	12
February	22	16
March	19	16
April	20	12
May	21	14

2. According to the table above, what was the total decrease from 1994 to 1995 in workday absences for the months shown?

   (A) 31
   (B) 30
   (C) 29
   (D) 28
   (E) 26

Choice **(B)** is correct. One approach is to find the total number of absences for each year for the months given, then compare the results. In 1994 the total was 100 and in 1995 it was 70. The decrease was $100 - 70$, which is 30.

3. A square is inscribed in a circle as shown in the figure above. What is the <u>least</u> number of lines that must be added to the figure so that the resulting figure consists of two right triangles inscribed in the circle?

    (A) One
    (B) Two
    (C) Three
    (D) Four
    (E) Five

Choice **(A)** is correct. If a single line connecting two opposite vertices of the square is added to the figure, it will divide the square into two right triangles. These right triangles will be inscribed in the circle because each of their vertices will lie on the circle.

Choice **(B)** is incorrect. For example, if both diagonals of the square are added to the figure, the resulting figure will indeed contain two right triangles inscribed in the circle. In fact, it will contain four such triangles. The second diagonal is not needed to form just two triangles.

4. A printing press produces 4,200 posters per hour. At this rate, in how many <u>minutes</u> can the printing press produce 840 posters?

    (A) 0.2
    (B) 1.5
    (C) 5
    (D) 12
    (E) 70

Choice **(D)** is correct. 4,200 posters in one hour is the same as 4,200 posters in 60 minutes, which is the same rate as 840 posters in x minutes. This information can be written as a proportion.

$$\frac{4200}{60} = \frac{840}{x} \quad \text{or} \quad \frac{70}{1} = \frac{840}{x}$$

Hence, $70x = 840$ and $x = 12$.

5. If $p = 3$, what is $4r(3 - 2p)$ in terms of r ?

   (A) $-12r$
   (B) $-8r$
   (C) $-7r$
   (D) $12r - 6$
   (E) $12r$

Choice **(A)** is correct. The expression $4r(3 - 2p)$ includes both variables p and r. By substituting 3 for p, you can obtain an expression in terms of r: $4r(3 - 2p) = 4r(3 - 6) = 4r(-3) = -12r$.

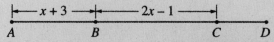

6. In the figure above, if the length of AD is $3x + 7$, what is the length of CD ?

   (A) $x + 2$
   (B) $x + 5$
   (C) 2
   (D) 4
   (E) 5

Choice **(E)** is correct. The length of AD is the sum of the lengths of AB, BC, and CD. You can state this fact algebraically with an equation: $3x + 7 = (x + 3) + (2x - 1) + n$ where n represents the length of CD.

Solve the equation for n.

$3x + 7 = x + 3 + 2x - 1 + n$
$3x + 7 = 3x + 2 + n$
$\quad 7 = 2 + n$
$\quad n = 5$

7. If r is 35 percent of p and s is 45 percent of p, what is $r + s$ in terms of p ?

   (A) $0.4p$
   (B) $0.5p$
   (C) $0.6p$
   (D) $0.7p$
   (E) $0.8p$

Choice **(E)** is correct. Since $r = 0.35p$ and $s = 0.45p$, $r + s = 0.35p + 0.45p = 0.8p$.

8. A bucket holds 4 quarts of popcorn. If $\frac{1}{3}$ cup of corn kernels makes 2 quarts of popcorn, how many buckets can be filled with the popcorn made from 4 cups of kernels?

(A) 96

(B) 24

(C) 6

(D) 3

(E) $1\frac{1}{2}$

Choice **(C)** is correct. If $\frac{1}{3}$ cup of corn kernels makes 2 quarts of popcorn, 1 cup of corn kernels will make 3 times that amount or 6 quarts of popcorn. At this rate, 4 cups of corn kernels will make 24 quarts of popcorn. Since each bucket holds 4 quarts of popcorn, it will be possible to fill $\frac{24}{4} = 6$ buckets with popcorn.

9. On a number line, if point P has coordinate -2 and point Q has coordinate 10, what is the coordinate of the point that is located $\frac{1}{4}$ of the way from P to Q ?

(A) $-1\frac{1}{2}$

(B) -1

(C) $-\frac{1}{2}$

(D) 1

(E) $2\frac{1}{2}$

Choice **(D)** is correct. Draw a number line placing point P at coordinate -2 and point Q at coordinate 10.

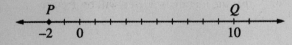

The distance between P and Q is 12 units. To determine the coordinate of the point located one-fourth of the way from P to Q, multiply: $12 \times \frac{1}{4} = 3$. The coordinate will be located 3 units to the right of P, and $-2 + 3 = 1$.

10. A group of s children has collected 650 bottle caps. If each child collects w more bottle caps per day for the next d days, which of the following represents the number of bottle caps that will be in the group's collection?

(A) $650sw$

(B) $650 + \dfrac{dw}{s}$

(C) $650 + \dfrac{ds}{w}$

(D) $650 + sw + d$

(E) $650 + dsw$

Choice **(E)** is correct. The group starts with 650 bottle caps. Since each child collects w more bottle caps per day for the next d days, each child collects dw more bottle caps. There are s children, each adding dw bottle caps to the collection, so a total of sdw bottle caps are added. Since $sdw = dsw$, the total is then $650 + sdw$, which is equivalent to $650 + dsw$.

11. Set T contains only the integers 1 through 50. If a number is selected at random from T, what is the probability that the number selected will be greater than 30 ?

(A) $\dfrac{1}{4}$

(B) $\dfrac{1}{3}$

(C) $\dfrac{2}{5}$

(D) $\dfrac{3}{5}$

(E) $\dfrac{2}{3}$

Choice **(C)** is correct. There are 50 integers in Set T, and 20 of them (the integers 31 through 50) are greater than 30. Therefore, if a number is selected at random from T, the probability is $\dfrac{20}{50}$ or $\dfrac{2}{5}$ that the number selected will be greater than 30.

Choice (D) is incorrect. This choice gives the probability that the number selected will NOT be greater than 30.

12. If an integer k is divisible by 2, 3, 6, and 9, what is the next larger integer divisible by these numbers?

   (A) $k + 6$
   (B) $k + 12$
   (C) $k + 18$
   (D) $k + 30$
   (E) $k + 36$

Choice (C) is correct. If k is divisible by 2, 3, 6, and 9, then k is a multiple of all these numbers. If n is the <u>smallest</u> number divisible by these four numbers, then the next larger integer after k that is divisible by the numbers is $k + n$. The smallest number divisible by 2, 3, 6, and 9 is $2 \times 3 \times 3$ or 18. So $k + 18$ is the answer.

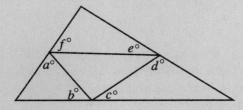

13. In the figure above, what is the value of $a + b + c + d + e + f$?

   (A) 180
   (B) 270
   (C) 360
   (D) 450
   (E) 540

Choice (C) is correct. Without additional information, it is not possible to determine the measure of any one of the labeled angles, but it is possible to determine their sum. Notice that the labeled angles all belong to three triangles. Label the other three angles of these triangles $x°$, $y°$, and $z°$, as shown below.

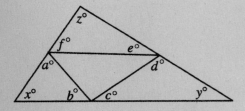

The sum of the angles in each of the three triangles is 180°; that is,

$a + b + x = 180$
$c + d + y = 180$
$e + f + z = 180$

Adding these, $a + b + x + c + d + y + e + f + z = 540$. The angles labeled $x°$, $y°$, and $z°$ are the three angles of the large triangle; hence $x + y + z = 180$. Subtract this equation from the previous one to get $a + b + c + d + e + f = 360$.

14. If x is $\frac{2}{3}$ of y and y is $\frac{3}{5}$ of z, what is the value of $\frac{x}{z}$?

    (A) $\frac{2}{5}$

    (B) $\frac{5}{8}$

    (C) $\frac{9}{10}$

    (D) $\frac{10}{9}$

    (E) $\frac{5}{2}$

Choice **(A)** is correct. Write "x is $\frac{2}{3}$ of y" as an expression for x in terms of y: $x = \frac{2}{3}y$. Write "y is $\frac{3}{5}$ of z" as an expression for y in terms of z: $y = \frac{3}{5}z$. If you substitute $\frac{3}{5}z$ for y in the equation $x = \frac{2}{3}y$, then $x = \frac{2}{3}\left(\frac{3}{5}z\right)$. Multiply the fractions and divide both sides of the equation by z to yield the value of $\frac{x}{z}$ as $\frac{2}{5}$. You must assume that $z \neq 0$; otherwise $\frac{x}{z}$ would be undefined.

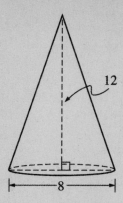

15. The right circular cone shown above is to be cut by a plane parallel to the base to form a new, smaller cone. If the diameter of the base of the smaller cone is 3, what is its height?

(A) 4
(B) 4.5
(C) 5
(D) 5.5
(E) 6

Choice **(B)** is correct.

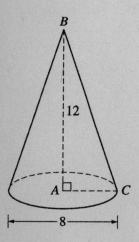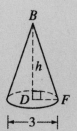

The larger cone was cut parallel to the base to form the smaller cone. Triangle *ABC*, formed by the radius *AC*, the altitude *AB*, and the slant height *BC* of the larger cone, is similar to triangle *DBF* of the smaller cone.

Corresponding sides of similar triangles are in proportion; therefore, $\dfrac{AB}{DB} = \dfrac{AC}{DF}$. Since *AC* and *DF* are radii, $AC = 4$ and

$DF = 1.5$. $\dfrac{AB}{DB} = \dfrac{AC}{DF}$, or $\dfrac{12}{h} = \dfrac{4}{1.5}$. Multiplying gives you $4h = 18$, and then dividing, $h = 4.5$. The height of the smaller cone is 4.5.

16. In how many different ways can 5 people arrange themselves in the 5 seats of a car for a trip if only 2 of the people can drive?

(A)   12
(B)   15
(C)   26
(D)   48
(E)   120

Choice **(D)** is correct. Since only 2 of the 5 people can drive, there are only 2 ways to fill the driver's seat. With the driver's seat filled, there are 4 passenger seats remaining. There are now 4 possible ways to assign someone to the first passenger seat. Next, there are 3 people remaining, so there are 3 ways to assign the second passenger seat. Similarly, there are 2 ways to assign the third passenger seat. Finally, with one person remaining, there is only 1 way to assign the fourth passenger seat. Therefore, by the multiplication principle, the total number of different arrangements is $2 \times (4 \times 3 \times 2 \times 1) = 48$.

17. If $2^x = 7$, then $2^{2x} =$

(A)   3.5
(B)   7
(C)   14
(D)   28
(E)   49

Choice **(E)** is correct. Since 2^{2x} is equal to $\left(2^x\right)^2$, you should square both sides of the given equation.

$$2^x = 7$$
$$\left(2^x\right)^2 = 7^2$$
$$2^{2x} = 49$$

Questions 18-20 refer to the following definition.

A positive integer is called a palindrome if it reads the same forward as it does backward. For example, 959 and 8228 are palindromes, whereas 1332 is not. Neither the first nor the last digit of a palindrome can be 0.

18. Which of the following integers is a palindrome?

    (A) 550
    (B) 2255
    (C) 2525
    (D) 2552
    (E) 5002

Choice **(D)** is correct. Since a palindrome is the same whether written forward or backward, you must find an answer choice that satisfies that condition. Notice that the definition rules out choice (A), since neither the first nor the last digit can be 0. In choice (D), the first and last digits are the same and the two middle digits are the same, so when the order of the digits is reversed the number is the same. No other choice has this property.

19. How many three-digit palindromes are there?

    (A) 19
    (B) 20
    (C) 90
    (D) 100
    (E) 810

Choice **(C)** is correct. In order for a three-digit integer to be a palindrome it must start and end with the same non-zero digit. There are 9 non-zero digits. The digit in the middle can be zero or any of the other digits, so there are 10 possibilities for the middle digit. The total number of possibilities is 9×10, which is 90. In constructing a palindrome, once the first digit is chosen, the third digit is determined, since it must be the same as the first digit. Overlooking this last point could lead you to the <u>incorrect</u> answer of $9 \times 10 \times 9 = 810$.

20. The next two palindromes greater than 50805 are m and p, where $m < p$. What is the value of $p - m$?

    (A) 10
    (B) 90
    (C) 100
    (D) 110
    (E) 210

Choice **(D)** is correct. To find the next two palindromes greater than 50805, you should increase some digits while making the number increase as little as possible. Recall that increasing the units digit 5 will force you to increase the first digit also, and this will increase the number quite a bit; 60806 is a big step up from 50805. A similar argument suggests that increasing the tens digit to 1 may not be the best thing to do either. Try increasing the middle digit, if possible. The next palindrome m after 50805 is 50905. Finding the next palindrome after 50905 will require a different strategy, since 9 is the largest digit. Increasing the two zero digits will produce a smaller increase than the two other digits, so the next palindrome p is 51015. The middle digit is dropped to zero to cause as little increase as possible. Since $m = 50905$ and $p = 51015$, the value of $p - m$ is 110.

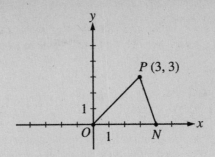

21. In the figure above, for which of the following coordinates of a point T (not shown) will $\triangle OTN$ have the same perimeter as $\triangle OPN$?

 (A) $(0, 3)$
 (B) $(1, 3)$
 (C) $(2, 3)$
 (D) $(4, 3)$
 (E) $(5, 3)$

Choice **(B)** is correct. If point T had coordinates $(1, 3)$, then OT would have the same length as PN and TN would have the same length as OP. Since the perimeter of $\triangle OTN$ is the sum of the lengths of OT, TN, and ON, and the perimeter of $\triangle OPN$ is the sum of the lengths of PN, OP, and ON, the perimeters of the two triangles would be equal. If point T had any of the other listed coordinates, then $\triangle OTN$ would have the same <u>area</u> as $\triangle OPN$ but not the same perimeter.

22. A person slices a pie into k equal pieces and eats one piece. In terms of k, what percent of the pie is left?

 (A) $100(k-1)\%$

 (B) $\dfrac{100(k-1)}{k}\%$

 (C) $\dfrac{100k}{k-1}\%$

 (D) $\dfrac{k-1}{100}\%$

 (E) $\dfrac{k-1}{100k}\%$

Choice **(B)** is correct. If one of k equal pieces of the pie is eaten, $k-1$ equal pieces are left. So $\dfrac{k-1}{k}$ is the fraction of the pie that is left. To convert $\dfrac{k-1}{k}$ to a percent, multiply the fraction by 100 and insert the percent symbol. Since "percent" means "per hundred," multiplying by 100 and inserting "%" does not change the value. Hence, $\dfrac{100(k-1)}{k}\%$ of the pie is left.

Choice **(E)** is incorrect. This is the result of dividing the fraction $\dfrac{k-1}{k}$ by 100 instead of multiplying it by 100 before the percent sign is inserted.

23. When each side of a given square is lengthened by 2 inches, the area is increased by 40 square inches. What is the length, in inches, of a side of the original square?

(A) 4
(B) 6
(C) 8
(D) 9
(E) 10

Choice **(D)** is correct. The quickest way to find the solution to this problem is to translate the given information into an equation and solve the equation. Let s represent the length of the side of the original square.

Then $(s+2)^2 = 40 + s^2$. Square the expression on the left-hand side of the equation and perform the following algebraic steps.

$$s^2 + 4s + 4 = 40 + s^2$$
$$4s + 4 = 40$$
$$4s = 36$$
$$s = 9$$

24. If a and b are positive, then the solution to the equation $\dfrac{bx}{a-x} = 1$ is $x =$

(A) $\dfrac{a}{b+1}$

(B) $\dfrac{a+1}{b+1}$

(C) $\dfrac{b-1}{a}$

(D) $\dfrac{b}{a+1}$

(E) $\dfrac{b+1}{a}$

Choice **(A)** is correct. The following algebraic steps lead to a solution.

$$\frac{bx}{a-x} = 1$$

$$bx = a - x$$
$$bx + x = a$$
$$(b+1)x = a$$

Since b is positive, $b+1$ is positive, and you can divide both sides of the equation by $b+1$ to get $x = \dfrac{a}{b+1}$

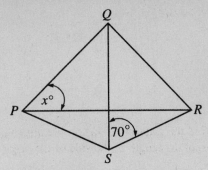

Note: Figure not drawn to scale.

25. In the quadrilateral above, if $PQ = SQ = RQ$ and $PS = SR$, then $x =$

   (A) 30
   (B) 40
   (C) 50
   (D) 60
   (E) 70

Choice **(C)** is correct. Although the figure may look 3-dimensional, the test directions say that all figures lie in a plane unless otherwise indicated. The use of the term quadrilateral also indicates a planar figure.

To find x, examine the triangles in the figure and use the fact that the sum of the measures of the three angles in a triangle is 180°.

Since $PQ = SQ = RQ$ and $PS = SR$, triangles PQS and SQR are congruent isosceles triangles and triangle PQR is isosceles. $\angle QSR$ and $\angle QRS$ each have a measure of 70°, so $\angle SQR$ has measure 40°. Then $\angle SQP$ has measure 40° too, and $\angle PQR$ has measure 80°. Therefore, in triangle PQR, angles QPR and QRP each have measure 50°. Hence, $x = 50$.

The note under the figure indicates that you should not judge the measure of the angles or the lengths of the sides of the triangles by their appearance: the drawing may be inaccurate. In this figure, for example, the triangle containing the $x°$ angle appears to be an isosceles right triangle, which would imply that $x = 45$. But $x \neq 45$, and 45 is not one of the choices. Sometimes it may be helpful to redraw the figure based on the given information.

Section 2

1. Although he can ------- isolated facts, he is no scholar: he is able to ------- information but cannot make sense of it.

   (A) regurgitate . . synthesize
   (B) memorize . . recite
   (C) falsify . . denounce
   (D) misinterpret . . acquire
   (E) recall . . disregard

Choice **(B)** is correct. The missing words in this sentence should contrast with the ideas of being a scholar and being able to make sense of information. *Memorize* and *recite* do this: *memorizing* isolated facts is not scholarly and *reciting* information is quite different from making sense out of it.

Choice (A) is incorrect. To *regurgitate* isolated facts is to repeat them without attention to meaning, which does contrast with the idea of being a scholar. But to *synthesize* is to combine diverse things into a coherent and often more complex whole. This word doesn't make sense when inserted in the sentence. If the person "cannot make sense of" information, then he could not combine such information into something more coherent and complex.

2. The use of tools among chimpanzees is learned behavior: young chimpanzees become ------- by ------- others.

   (A) socialized . . overcoming
   (B) dominant . . obeying
   (C) vocal . . mimicking
   (D) adept . . imitating
   (E) agile . . following

Choice **(D)** is correct. The colon indicates that the second part of the sentence will help to explain or clarify the first part. *Adept* means skilled. If the use of tools among chimpanzees were learned behavior, then it would make sense to say that young chimpanzees become *adept*, or skilled, by *imitating* others.

Choice (C) is incorrect. *Mimicking* makes sense when inserted in the sentence because a chimpanzee might easily learn something by *mimicking*, or *imitating*, others. But *vocal* does not logically follow from the first part of the sentence: being *vocal* has nothing to do with using physical tools. Remember, both words must make sense in the sentence for the answer to be correct.

3. The speech was a ------- of random and contradictory information that could not be integrated into -------, consistent whole.

   (A) collage . . a rambling
   (B) development . . an ambiguous
   (C) hodgepodge . . a coherent
   (D) morass . . an amorphous
   (E) harangue . . an unintelligible

Choice **(C)** is correct. A *hodgepodge* is a mix of dissimilar things. *Coherent* means logically ordered, possessing clarity and intelligibility. "Random and contradictory information" can rightfully be characterized as a *hodgepodge*. It is reasonable, then, to say that a *hodgepodge* could not be integrated into a logically ordered and intelligible whole.

Choice (B) is incorrect. *Ambiguous* means unclear, or open to multiple interpretations. This word contradicts the meaning of the sentence; you cannot integrate something into a whole that is both *ambiguous* and "consistent." Also, it would be odd to speak of a "*development* of random and contradictory information" since the word *development* suggests an ordered evolution.

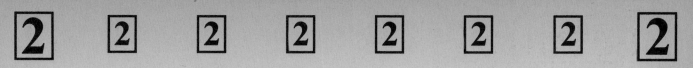

4. The prosecutor termed the defendants' actions ------- because there was no justification for their intentional disregard for the law.

   (A) **indefensible**
   (B) surreptitious
   (C) indefatigable
   (D) comprehensive
   (E) corrective

Choice **(A)** is correct. The word "because" indicates that the second part of the sentence will explain why the defendants' actions were described the way they were. *Indefensible* means incapable of being justified or excused. If there was "no justification" for the defendants' actions, then they could be characterized as *indefensible*.

Choice (B) is incorrect. *Surreptitious* means marked by stealth. To do something *surreptitiously* is to do it furtively, unobtrusively, or secretively. While the defendants' actions may in fact have been *surreptitious*, this word doesn't fit the logic of the sentence as it is written. You would not call the actions *surreptitious* because there was "no justification" for them; you would only call them *surreptitious* because they were done secretively.

5. Acid rain is damaging lakes in ------- way, causing the virtually unnoticed ------- of these aquatic ecosystems.

   (A) a manifest . . eradication
   (B) a nefarious . . polarization
   (C) **an insidious . . destruction**
   (D) a methodical . . amalgamation
   (E) an obvious . . stagnation

Choice **(C)** is correct. *Insidious* means working in a subtly harmful manner. *Insidious* and *destruction* make sense when inserted in the sentence: if acid rain is causing "virtually unnoticed *destruction*" of lakes, then it can be said to be damaging them in an *insidious*, or subtle, way.

Choice (A) is incorrect. *Eradication* is the complete removal or elimination of something. *Eradication* makes only limited sense when inserted in the second blank—the sentence says that the ecosystem is being damaged, not eliminated. Inserting *manifest*, which means obvious, in the first blank would contradict the meaning of the sentence, since the damage is virtually unnoticed, not obvious.

6. The new concert hall proved to be a -------: it was costly, acoustically unsatisfactory, and far too small.

   (A) colossus
   (B) milestone
   (C) **debacle**
   (D) consecration
   (E) fabrication

Choice **(C)** is correct. A *debacle* is a complete failure. The sentence states that the new concert hall was expensive to build, characterized by bad acoustics, and too small. Since the concert hall was unsatisfactory in so many ways, it can be described as a *debacle*.

Choice (E) is incorrect. A *fabrication* refers to something that has been assembled or is a misrepresentation. The sentence does not infer that the concert hall was to be made a particular way or how much it should have cost, so it could not be misrepresented. Both of these meanings also fail to establish the idea that the concert hall was unsatisfactory in so many important ways.

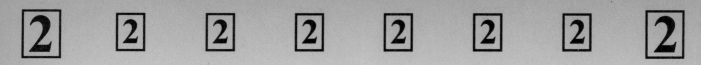

7. A hypocrite may ------- reprehensible acts but escape discovery by affecting -------.

   (A) abhor . . profundity
   (B) condone . . enthusiasm
   (C) commit . . innocence
   (D) perform . . immorality
   (E) condemn . . repentance

Choice **(C)** is correct. A "hypocrite" is a person who practices hypocrisy, which is the feigning of beliefs or virtues that one does not actually possess. Actions that are "reprehensible", or blamable, are worthy of condemnation. These words make sense when inserted in the sentence: "a hypocrite might *commit* terrible acts but avoid discovery by affecting *innocence*."

Choice (D) is incorrect. Although the word *perform* is logical in the context of the sentence because a hypocrite might well perform reprehensible acts, the second word, *immorality*, is not. A hypocrite would pretend to be virtuous, not immoral. Also, it does not make sense to say that a person who performed reprehensible acts "affected," or put up a pretense of, *immorality* since reprehensible acts are by definition immoral.

8. The review was -------, recounting the play's felicities and its flaws without unduly emphasizing one or the other.

   (A) equitable
   (B) immoderate
   (C) cumulative
   (D) unproductive
   (E) adulatory

Choice **(A)** is correct. "Felicities" are things that make one happy—in this case, aspects of the play that are stylistically appropriate or pleasing. *Equitable* means evenhanded or impartial. If the review described "the play's felicities and its flaws without unduly emphasizing one over the other," then it could be characterized as evenhanded or impartial.

Choice (C) is incorrect. *Cumulative* has the same root as the more familiar word "accumulation." To say something is *cumulative* means that it has increased through successive additions. This word might at first seem appealing because the review is said to describe a number of things ("the play's felicities and flaws"), but the review did not accumulate these things through a series of successive additions.

9. Rosita Perú, who rose to become the highest-ranking female in the television industry, was ------- recruited: Spanish language program-producers courted her persistently.

   (A) indiscriminately
   (B) enigmatically
   (C) vicariously
   (D) rancorously
   (E) assiduously

Choice **(E)** is correct. *Assiduously*, in this context, means persistently. To "court" is to try to favorably gain the attentions of, or to win the affections of someone. The colon indicates that the material in the second part of the sentence will help to explain or clarify what has come before it. Since the producers courted Perú persistently, it makes sense to say that she was *assiduously* recruited.

Choice (C) is incorrect. The word *vicarious* is used to describe things that are experienced through imaginative participation in another person's experience. The sentence suggests that the producers actually sought to recruit Perú, not that they somehow did it through imaginative participation.

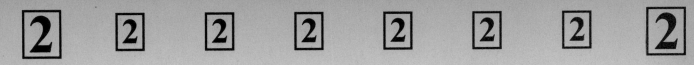

10. LUBRICANT : SLIDE ::

   (A) battery : discharge
   (B) glue : adhere
   (C) stain : cleanse
   (D) poison : ingest
   (E) water : drink

Choice **(B)** is correct. A LUBRICANT is a substance that is used to reduce friction between moving parts. A LUBRICANT is used to make things SLIDE, just as *glue* is used to make things *adhere*, or stick together.

Choice (E) is incorrect. *Water* is something a person might *drink*, but you would not say that the purpose of *water* is to make things *drink*.

11. STOMP : WALK ::

   (A) devour : starve
   (B) shout : speak
   (C) run : scamper
   (D) prepare : finish
   (E) deliberate : conclude

Choice **(B)** is correct. To STOMP is to tread heavily or noisily. To STOMP is to WALK noisily, just as to *shout* is to *speak* noisily.

Choice (C) is incorrect. To *scamper* is to *run* quickly, lightly, and often playfully. It would not be accurate to say that to *run* is to *scamper* noisily.

12. INDEX : TOPICS ::

   (A) agenda : meeting
   (B) diary : secrets
   (C) roster : names
   (D) manual : equipment
   (E) ledger : numbers

Choice **(C)** is correct. An INDEX is a list of TOPICS or bibliographic entries. A *roster* is a list, typically of people's *names*. An INDEX is a list of TOPICS, just as a *roster* is a list of *names*.

Choice (B) is incorrect. A *diary* is a journal, a place where a person records experiences and ideas. A person might choose to write *secrets* in a *diary*, but a *diary* is not a list of *secrets*.

13. MENDICANT : BEG ::

   (A) sycophant : demean
   (B) braggart : boast
   (C) parasite : contribute
   (D) hero : worship
   (E) dissembler : believe

Choice **(B)** is correct. A MENDICANT is a BEGgar. A *braggart* is a person who speaks in a self-admiring way. A MENDICANT by definition BEGs, just as a *braggart* by definition *boasts*.

Choice (D) is incorrect. A *hero* is a person who is noted for courage or for some special achievement. People might *worship* a *hero*, but you could not say a *hero* by definition *worships*.

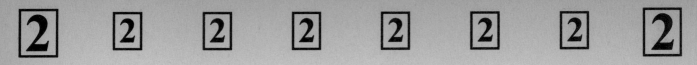

14. PRUDENT : INDISCRETION ::

(A) **frugal : wastefulness**
(B) proud : accomplishment
(C) generous : wealth
(D) disqualified : competition
(E) disgruntled : cynicism

Choice **(A)** is correct. PRUDENT means marked by wisdom or good judgment. A person who is PRUDENT would consider all circumstances and possible outcomes before acting. INDISCRETION refers to a lack of sound judgment or self-restraint in speech or behavior. *Frugal* means careful in the use of money or material resources. One who is PRUDENT avoids INDISCRETION, just as one who is *frugal* avoids *wastefulness*.

Choice **(E)** is incorrect. *Disgruntled* means discontented. *Cynicism* is an attitude characterized by a distrust of human nature and human motives. Although being *disgruntled* might result from *cynicism*, you would not say that to be *disgruntled* is to avoid *cynicism*.

15. VISCOUS : FLOW ::

(A) transparent : see
(B) stationary : stop
(C) arid : rain
(D) **stiff : bend**
(E) damp : soak

Choice **(D)** is correct. The word VISCOUS is used to characterize fluids that do not FLOW easily, such as molasses or motor oil. Something that is VISCOUS does not FLOW easily, just as something that is *stiff* does not *bend* easily.

Choice **(B)** is incorrect. Something that is *stationary* does not move or is incapable of moving. When something has come to a complete *stop*, it is said to be *stationary*. It doesn't make sense to say that something *stationary* does not *stop* easily, since it is already *stopped*.

16. According to Navajo tradition, the most significant perspective on a sandpainting is that of the

(A) group that requests the sandpainting's creation
(B) persons represented by the sandpainting figures
(C) Navajo leader conducting the sandpainting rite
(D) artists who conceive and design the sandpainting
(E) **person for whom the sandpainting is made**

Choice **(E)** is correct. This choice is the best response because it is directly supported by the information in the passage. In lines 21–32, the author describes the purpose of Navajo sandpaintings: they are "instruments of a ritual process" in which "a person in need of healing is symbolically remade in a way corresponding to his or her ailment." Later, in lines 46–49, the author connects the purpose of sandpaintings to the way they are meant to be viewed, stating that the "most important point of view is that of the person for whom the painting is made, and this person sees the painting from the inside out because he or she sits in the middle of it."

Choice **(D)** is incorrect. Although an artist's perspective is considered important in many traditions, the passage does not indicate that it is important in Navajo sandpainting.

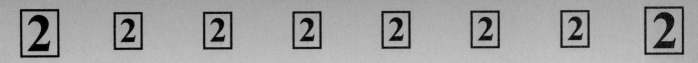

17. As used in line 8, "deepened" most nearly means

    (A) darkened
    (B) heightened
    (C) immersed
    (D) made distant
    (E) made obscure

Choice **(B)** is correct. In the first paragraph, the author writes that "when our understanding of art is heavily focused on objects, we tend to look in the wrong place for art," and adds in the next paragraph that "the concerns I have are deepened as I begin to compare how we, as outsiders, view sandpaintings…." The author, then, has identified a concern and noted how that concern has "deepened," or grown stronger. To *heighten* means to increase or make more intense. Thus, "deepened" most nearly means *heightened* in this context.

Choice (A) is incorrect. Although the word "deepened" can, in some contexts, mean *darkened* (as in made more obscure), nothing suggests that the author's concerns became more obscure—if anything, they became clearer.

18. What would happen if Navajo practices regarding sandpaintings (lines 14–20) were strictly observed?

    (A) Only the Navajo would be permitted to exhibit sandpaintings as works of art.
    (B) All sandpaintings would be destroyed before the rite of re-creation.
    (C) The sandpaintings could be viewed only during the sandpainting rite.
    (D) The sand-glue craft would be the only art form in which figures from sandpaintings could appear.
    (E) The Navajo would be able to focus exclusively on the sandpaintings' images of unity.

Choice **(C)** is correct. The primary point of the passage is that sandpaintings should be appreciated as "instruments of a ritual process" (lines 21–22), not as aesthetic objects. That is, they are not meant to be simply looked at, but to perform a function. In keeping with this, the "Navajo strictly forbid making representations of sandpaintings," and their tradition demands that they be destroyed by "sundown on the day they are made" (lines 14–20). If these Navajo practices were to be strictly observed, *the sandpaintings could only be viewed during the actual sandpainting rite*.

Choice (B) is incorrect. As the passage makes clear, sandpaintings are created during the rite of re-creation and are destroyed afterward. They could not be destroyed <u>before</u> the rite occurs.

19. Why did the Navajo listeners mentioned in line 39 laugh?

    (A) It would be dangerous for a person to climb onto the roof of a hogan.
    (B) The view from the periphery is more amusing than the view from the center of the paintings.
    (C) Only the person in need of healing should act in the way suggested by the author.
    (D) Critical details in the sandpaintings would be imperceptible from such a distance.
    (E) A bird's-eye perspective is irrelevant to the intended function of the paintings.

Choice **(E)** is correct. The passage as a whole compares Navajo to non-Navajo ways of viewing sandpaintings. In lines 33–38, the author asserts that "In terms of visual perspective, we [non-Navajo readers] traditionally view sandpainting from a position as if we were directly above and at such a distance that the whole painting is immediately graspable," but for the Navajo, "this view is completely impossible." The author does not mean, of course, that it is physically impossible for the Navajo to view a sandpainting this way. Rather, it is "impossible" in the sense that the Navajo believe that the "most important point of view is that of the person for whom the painting is made" (lines 46–47). This person sits in the center of the painting and sees it from the inside out. So when the author proposes viewing the painting from the roof of the hogan, the Navajo listeners laugh: they believe that such *a bird's-eye perspective is irrelevant to the function of the painting*.

Choice (D) is incorrect. The author suggests that for non-Navajo people, paintings are traditionally viewed from a point where "the whole painting is immediately graspable," and implies that looking through the "roof of a hogan" might afford such a view. Looking at a sandpainting from this vantage would presumably allow one to see it very well. It is unlikely that *critical details* in such a large painting *would be imperceptible from such a distance*.

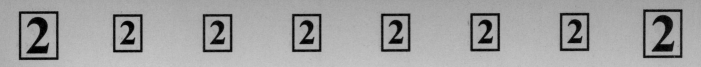

20. The phrase "obvious aesthetic value" (line 60) suggests that

   (A) despite an attempt to separate sandpaintings from the realm of art, the author recognizes their artistic qualities
   (B) imposing artistic rules on sandpaintings diminishes their symbolic value
   (C) the Navajo believe the sandpaintings' artistic qualities to be as important as their function
   (D) the author discourages artistic elitism, yet acknowledges the esteemed reputation that sandpainters enjoy within the Navajo community
   (E) aesthetic value should be associated with objects of natural beauty as well as with things created by humans

Choice (A) is correct. Throughout the passage, the author argues that sandpaintings must be understood in the context in which they are created, not simply as objects of art. In lines 57–61, the author even suggests that it is the "wisdom of the Navajo" that sandpaintings be destroyed in their use, so that their "obvious aesthetic value … does not supplant [replace] the human or cosmic concern." The phrase "obvious aesthetic value" indicates that the author is recognizing the artistic qualities of these paintings even while arguing that they must be understood in contexts other than the realm of art. Choice (A) comes closest to expressing this idea.

Choice (B) is incorrect. The author does not address the possibility of *imposing artistic rules* on sandpaintings. The author is only concerned with the ways that people respond to these works of art once they have been created.

21. The author's discussion of artists' palettes (lines 62–69) emphasizes the

   (A) array of colors in the creation of sandpaintings
   (B) insight required to appreciate technically unique art
   (C) growing legitimacy of sandpainting reproductions
   (D) value of sandpaintings as a means rather than an end
   (E) benefit of combining several components to produce a single painting

Choice (D) is correct. In lines 62–69, the author argues that "the confinement of our attention to the reproduction of sandpaintings" is like hanging "paint-covered artists' palettes on the wall to admire." A palette is a board on which an artist mixes colors while painting. The comparison of a palette to a sandpainting is apt: a palette is a means used to create a painting, just as sandpainting is a means (an "instrument in a creative process") used to create a "healthy human being" (line 56). To focus on an artist's palette would be to treat the means by which a painting is created as though it were the intended end. Similarly, to focus on a reproduction of a sandpainting would be to value the means as an end. And this, the author concludes in the final sentence, would be "foolishly missing the point." Instead, people should *value sandpaintings as a means rather than an end*.

Choice (B) is incorrect. This choice indicates that the point of the discussion is that insight is required to appreciate technically unique art. The author does not, however, make the point that sandpaintings are *technically unique*; indeed, the author does not discuss the technical qualities of these paintings at all. Moreover, the discussion of the artists' palettes does not emphasize the idea that *insight* is *required* to appreciate art.

22. The information in the passage suggests that a museum's exhibition of reproduced Navajo sandpaintings would

   (A) undermine the effectiveness of sandpaintings in the healing process
   (B) help to safeguard the traditions and treasures of Navajo civilization
   (C) devalue the representations of sandpainting figures in the sand-glue craft
   (D) discourage non-Navajo people from preserving actual sandpaintings
   (E) perpetuate the importance of a painting's form rather than its function

Choice (E) is correct. In lines 55–57, the author explains that a sandpainting is not intended to be the "product" or end result of the creative process; rather, the intended result is a "healthy human being or the re-creation of a well-ordered world." In lines 57–60, the author indicates that the Navajo are wise to destroy sandpaintings because this ensures that the paintings themselves aren't valued more than the human results they are supposed to produce. We can infer from these lines that preserving reproduced Navajo paintings in a museum would produce the undesirable result of *perpetuating the importance of the painting's form* (the actual painting itself) *rather than its function* (to make a human being healthy or to re-create a well-ordered world).

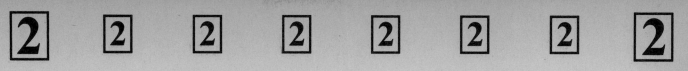

Choice (B) is incorrect. Although this answer might appear to make sense because the customary role of museums is to preserve the traditions and treasures of civilizations, the passage clearly states that sandpaintings are "not aesthetic objects; they are instruments of a ritual process," and that this is why they are "destroyed by sundown on the day they are made" (lines 20–22). To preserve a sandpainting, the author states, would be like hanging "paint-covered artists' palettes" on a wall—it would be "foolishly missing the point" (lines 62—69). Choice (B) is wrong because an exhibition of reproduced Navajo sandpaintings would not help to safeguard a Navajo tradition, but would actually cause one to ignore the tradition and focus on the object's aesthetic qualities.

23. Which of the following would the author consider to be most similar to a non-Navajo person's appreciation of sandpainting, as it is discussed in the passage?

 (A) Savoring the taste of a cake that someone else has baked
 (B) Enjoying a book written by an anonymous author
 (C) Admiring an ancient structure without comprehending its historical context
 (D) Praising a concert performance without knowing how to play a musical instrument
 (E) Appreciating a building without having contributed to its construction

Choice **(C)** is correct. The introduction indicates that this passage is written by a scholar trying to interpret Navajo traditions for non-Navajo readers. The passage begins with the assertion that non-Navajo people "cannot fully appreciate some Native American objects [they] consider art without also appreciating the contexts in which they are produced." The author implies that non-Navajo people tend to admire reproductions of sandpaintings as "objects" in and of themselves, and to ignore the context in which they were created. Choice (C) most resembles this way of looking at sandpaintings because it involves admiring an unfamiliar aesthetic object without considering the circumstances in which it was created.

Choice (D) is incorrect. While knowing how to play a musical instrument may enhance one's appreciation of a concert, it would not necessarily give one an understanding of the historical context which gave rise to music that is performed. Choice (D), while appealing, is not as good as choice (C).

24. Which statement best summarizes the author's perspective on the appreciation of sandpainting?

 (A) We should not revere ceremonial art objects because such reverence is a kind of tyranny that stifles the full expression of ideas.
 (B) We must understand that the materials of the object and the design it takes are at the core of its meaning.
 (C) We cannot fully understand sandpaintings until we witness their healing powers.
 (D) We must understand the process by which an object was created and the purpose it serves in order to grasp its significance.
 (E) Our usual way of looking at art objects should be augmented by knowledge of the artists' personal history.

Choice **(D)** is correct. The author states in the very first sentence of the passage that one cannot fully appreciate some Native American art works without "appreciating the context in which they are produced." The second paragraph then focuses on Navajo sandpaintings and provides some context for their creation, explaining that they are created in a "ritual process" in which a person "in need of healing is symbolically remade in a way corresponding to his or her ailment." The third paragraph explains how this influences the perspective by which these paintings were meant to be viewed. The final paragraph reiterates the idea that a sandpainting is "but an instrument for the creative act" and to focus too much on reproductions of sandpaintings is to miss the point. Choice (D), then, best summarizes the author's perspective on the appreciation of sandpainting: one must understand the process of creation and the purpose of sandpaintings in order to grasp their significance.

Choice (B) is not correct. To focus on the materials from which a sandpainting is made, and the design it takes, would be to focus on the work itself, rather than its context. This is the precise opposite of the author's perspective.

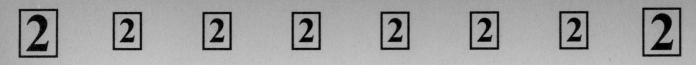

25. The primary purpose of the passage is to

    (A) evaluate women's travel books and journals from a literary perspective
    (B) contrast nineteenth-century women travelers with male explorers of the same period
    (C) describe changes in travel opportunities for wealthy women in the nineteenth century
    (D) examine the motives that some nineteenth-century women had for traveling
    (E) analyze the historical significance of women travelers' books and journals

Choice **(D)** is correct. In the first paragraph, the author indicates that the "real destination" (line 10) of women travelers "was a restorative idea rather than a place on the map" (lines 11–12). In the third paragraph, the author asks "What, *specifically*, were these women seeking 'abroad'?" (lines 22–23), then argues that women sought an "emotional outlet" (lines 26–27) through travel. Paragraph 4 explains that travel appealed to women as a means to improve intellectually. Paragraph 5 suggests that later generations of women travelers were "impelled by essentially the same impetus" (lines 59–60) as their predecessors. The passage is primarily focused on examining *the motives that some nineteenth century women had for traveling*.

Choice **(E)** is incorrect. Although the passage does conclude with an observation about the importance of women's travel books for the emancipation of women, this comes as something of an afterthought and is not the main focus of the passage. Moreover, the historical significance of such documents is not closely analyzed.

26. In line 2, "iron hoops" primarily signify the

    (A) strict codes governing the social behavior of women
    (B) unbecoming styles of Victorian fashion
    (C) lack of mobility within society
    (D) household implements disdained by Victorian women
    (E) barriers to a woman's right to travel alone

Choice **(A)** is correct. In the first sentence of the passage, the author observes that privileged women of the nineteenth century were restricted by the "iron hoops of convention" (line 2). The phrase "of convention" indicates that the "iron hoops" symbolize the conventional rules or codes of conduct that society expects its members to obey. In this particular case, the rules must have been quite strict since women are said to have been "immobilized" by them. Thus, the "iron hoops" of line 2 signify *strict codes governing the social behavior of women*.

Choice **(C)** is incorrect. The first sentence of the passage suggests that women were "immobilized" by "iron hoops" only in the sense that they were subject to gender-based limitations on their freedom. There is no indication that women were unable to move freely across the boundaries that separated one social class from another.

27. The main reason certain women traveled abroad during the nineteenth century was to

    (A) seek the companionship of like-minded women
    (B) satisfy a desire for freedom and adventure
    (C) explore remote and uncharted places
    (D) research and publish travel guides
    (E) visit countries about which they had only read

Choice **(B)** is correct. In the third paragraph, the author observes that privileged women of the nineteenth century were anxious for an "emotional outlet," which they found through traveling (lines 26–27). The author then explains that during their travels these women could enjoy a sense of "freedom of action and thought" denied to them at home, while experiencing "adventure" of the sort that they had only read about in novels (lines 30–32).

Choice **(C)** is incorrect. While acknowledging that women's travels sometimes led them to "remote places" (lines 14–15) like those that men were often eager to explore, the author explicitly states that women had "little intent to imitate the male fashion for exploration." According to the author, "discovery was not the aim of most women travelers" (lines 18–19).

28. In line 62, "crystallized" most nearly means

   (A) refracted
   (B) metamorphosed
   (C) glittered
   (D) sharpened
   (E) solidified

Choice **(E)** is correct. To "crystallize" means to assume a solid form or *solidify*. For example, "crystallized" may be applied to water that has literally *solidified* into ice or, more metaphorically, to an idea that has taken solid shape in one's mind. In the final paragraph of the passage, the author uses this word to describe how the "independence and enlightenment" (lines 60–61) experienced by women travelers took shape, or *solidified*, as guiding principles in the cause for women's rights.

Choice (D) is incorrect. "Crystallize" does not mean *sharpen* in ordinary use, nor does this meaning fit the context of the passage. It makes little sense to say that the forces of independence and enlightenment grew *sharp* in the movement for equal rights.

29. In what way was a certain type of travel book an "instrument" (lines 64–65)?

   (A) It conveyed an impression of beauty.
   (B) It revealed what would otherwise have been hidden.
   (C) It was an agent that helped bring about a change.
   (D) It registered a cataclysmic change in society.
   (E) It was an implement wielded by an expert.

Choice **(C)** is correct. In the final sentence of the passage, the nineteenth-century woman's travel book is described as an "important instrument for the emancipation of women" (lines 64–65). An "instrument" is something that aids in the performance of an action, so it is implied that the travel book somehow aided in the emancipation of women. This emancipation—the process whereby women were granted a greater degree of freedom than in times past—constituted an important social change. Thus, the author is suggesting that the travel book served as a catalyst or agent that helped bring about a change in the social standing of women.

Choice (B) is incorrect. The woman's travel book was undoubtedly revealing in some way and therefore instrumental in bringing to light what may otherwise have been hidden, but the qualifying phrase "for the emancipation of women" makes it clear that the author thinks of the travel book specifically as a liberating force and not simply as a means of disclosure.

30. The author's conclusion would be most directly supported by additional information that

   (A) described the details of particular journeys of women travelers
   (B) revealed the number and titles of travel journals published by women
   (C) indicated how nineteenth-century travel writers influenced the future status of women
   (D) discussed the accuracy of the travel information included in women's journals and books
   (E) discussed the effect of nineteenth-century travel writers on modern women writers

Choice **(C)** is correct. The author concludes in lines 64–65 that travel writers influenced the status of women in such a way as to bring about their eventual liberation: "the once-lowly travel book rather unexpectedly became an important instrument for the emancipation of women." But the author does not explain <u>how</u> this influence worked. To support the conclusion directly, the author would need to provide a specific example or general explanation indicating exactly *how nineteenth-century travel writers influenced the future status of women*.

Choice (A) is incorrect. Describing the details of particular journeys made by women travelers might give the reader a better idea of the type of material included in travel books, which might help the reader to understand the potentially liberating effects of these books. However, these details would not <u>directly</u> support the author's conclusion that such books were in fact instrumental in the emancipation of women.

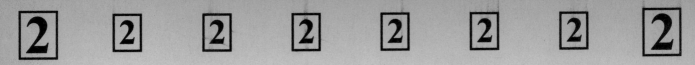

31. The author suggests that the travel books written by nineteenth-century women are significant primarily because they

   (A) reflect the expanding role women were soon to assume in Britain and America
   (B) were "once-lowly" and are now prized by book collectors
   (C) helped women to achieve economic independence
   (D) were richly illustrated and helped to educate people about life abroad
   (E) are valuable historical sources that describe nineteenth-century travel

Choice **(A)** is correct. In the last paragraph, the author observes that the personal narratives contained in travel books written by nineteenth-century women "combined genuine learning with the spirit of individualism" (lines 56–57). The author then argues that these two personal qualities (summed up in lines 60–61 as "independence and enlightenment") were adopted by later generations of women as goals of the movement for equal rights. The eventual success of that movement, i.e., the "emancipation of women" (line 65), would therefore bring independence and enlightenment to British and American women, and this, in turn, would expand their role in society.

Choice (C) is incorrect. Although the travel books are said to have played a role in advancing the cause of women's independence quite generally, there is no indication anywhere in the passage that this independence was of a specifically "economic" nature.

$$3n - 6 = 21$$

1.

n	5

Choice **(A)** is correct. If $3n - 6 = 21$, then $3n = 27$ and $n = 9$. The quantity in Column A is greater than the quantity in Column B.

2.

The average (arithmetic mean) of 3, 4, and 5	The average (arithmetic mean) of 2, 3, 7, and 8

Choice **(B)** is correct. The average of the numbers in Column A is $\dfrac{3+4+5}{3} = 4$, the average of the numbers in Column B is

$\dfrac{2+3+7+8}{4} = 5$, and $4 < 5$.

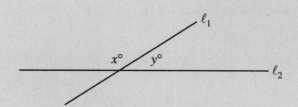

Note: Figure not drawn to scale.

$$x > 90$$

3.

y	30

Choice **(D)** is correct. Since x and y are supplementary angles, $x + y = 180$. If $x > 90$, then $y < 90$. Although $y < 90$, it is not necessarily true that y is equal to 30. Since y could have any value between 0 and 90, the relationship between y and 30 cannot be determined from the information given.

Choice (C) is incorrect. Although y appears in the figure to have a value close to 30, the figure is not drawn to scale. Even if it were drawn to scale, there is not enough information to determine the value of y.

r, s, t, and u are consecutive integers.

$$r < s < t < u$$

4.

| $r + u$ | $s + t$ |

Choice **(C)** is correct. Since r, s, t, and u are consecutive integers and $r < s < t < u$, you can write all of the integers in terms of r. That is, $s = r + 1$, $t = r + 2$, and $u = r + 3$. Then $r + u = r + (r + 3) = 2r + 3$ and $s + t = (r + 1) + (r + 2) = 2r + 3$. The quantities in Column A and Column B are equal.

Ian has x dollars in a savings account.

$$x > 0$$

5.

| Twice the number of dollars that Ian has in the account | $200x$ |

Choice **(B)** is correct. If Ian has x dollars in his account, twice that is $2x$, the quantity in Column A. Since x is a positive number, $200x > 2x$.

Choice (C) is incorrect. Misinterpreting Column B to mean 200% of x would produce this incorrect choice.

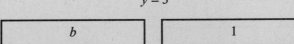

6.

| b | 1 |

Choice **(D)** is correct. Substituting the given values of x and y, you can obtain the equation $a + b = 3$. Since there is no more information given about a or b, the value of b cannot be determined. For example, $a = 1$ and $b = 2$ satisfy the equation and so do $a = 2$ and $b = 1$.

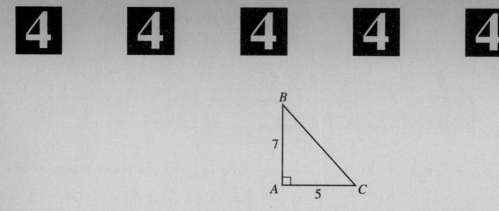

7.

| The length of BC | | 9 |

Choice **(B)** is correct. Since $\triangle ABC$ is a right triangle, you can use the Pythagorean Theorem. $BC = \sqrt{5^2 + 7^2} = \sqrt{74}$. Since $\sqrt{74} < \sqrt{81} = 9$, the length of BC is less than 9. The value of $\sqrt{74}$ is not needed to answer this question.

$$(x-3)(x+2) < 0$$

8.

| x | | 3 |

Choice **(B)** is correct. Since the product of the two quantities $(x-3)$ and $(x+2)$ is negative, one of the quantities must be negative and the other positive. Since $(x-3)$ is less than $(x+2)$, $(x-3)$ must be the negative quantity. If $x - 3 < 0$, then $x < 3$ and the quantity in Column B is greater than the quantity in Column A.

$$\begin{array}{r} PW \\ -WP \\ \hline 72 \end{array}$$

P and W represent different nonzero digits in the correctly solved subtraction problem.

9.

| P | | W |

Choice **(A)** is correct. You know that P and W are different digits from 1 to 9. Since the answer to the subtraction problem, 72, is positive, you also know that PW is greater than WP, which means P must be greater than W.

Note: It is not necessary to find specific values for P and W, but you can find possible values using some algebra. The value of the 2-digit number PW can be written as $10P + W$. Similarly for WP. Therefore,

$$(10P + W) - (10W + P) = 72$$
$$10P + W - 10W - P = 72$$
$$9P - 9W = 72$$
$$9(P - W) = 72$$
$$P - W = 8$$

The only two digits P and W that satisfy this last equation are 9 and 1. Hence, PW represents 91 and WP represents 19.

u, v, and w are positive numbers.

10.

| $u + v + w$ | uvw |

Choice **(D)** is correct. If $u = v = w = \frac{1}{4}$, then $u + v + w = \frac{3}{4}$ and $uvw = \frac{1}{64}$, and the quantity in Column A is greater than the quantity in Column B. If, however, $u = v = w = 2$, then $u + v + w = 6$, and $uvw = 8$, so the quantity in Column B is greater than the quantity in Column A. This means that the relationship cannot be determined from the information given.

Choice **(B)** is incorrect. The first example above shows that the product of three numbers is not always greater than their sum.

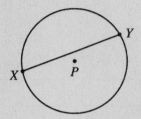

The circle has center P and area 5π.

11.

| The length of XY | 5 |

Choice **(B)** is correct. Since the area of a circle is given by the formula $A = \pi r^2$ and the area of this circle is 5π, $r^2 = 5$ and the radius is $\sqrt{5}$. Hence, a diameter, which is the longest chord in the circle, has length $2\sqrt{5}$. Chord XY is not a diameter of the circle since it does not pass through the center of the circle. Therefore, the length of XY is less than $2\sqrt{5}$. Since $2\sqrt{5} < 5$, the length of XY is less than 5.

$$x = y + 1$$
x is a positive odd integer.

12.

| $2x$ | $3y - 1$ |

Choice **(D)** is correct. Since you have to compare $2x$ to an expression in y, multiply both sides of the given equation by 2. $2x = 2(y + 1) = 2y + 2$. The expression in Column A is the same as $2y + 2$. How does $2y + 2$ in Column A compare to $3y - 1$ in Column B? If you add 1 to both columns, you have $2y + 3$ and $3y$. If you then subtract $2y$ from both quantities, you are left with 3 and y. Since x is a positive odd integer, y must be an even integer. But is it greater than or less than 3? There is not enough information to determine that because y could be 0, 2, 4, 6, etc.

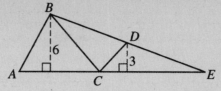

Note: Figure not drawn to scale.

$$AE = 27$$
$$AC = 9$$

13.

The area of $\triangle ABC$	The area of $\triangle CDE$

Choice **(C)** is correct. The area of a triangle is equal to one-half the base times the altitude. For Column A, the altitude of $\triangle ABC$ is 6 and the base is 9, so the area is $\frac{1}{2} \times 9 \times 6 = 27$. For Column B, the altitude of $\triangle CDE$ is 3 and the base is 18. The length 18 of the base is found by subtracting 9, the length of AC, from 27, the length of AE. So the area is $\frac{1}{2} \times 18 \times 3 = 27$.

Note that in this question, the triangles may not appear to have the same area, but the figure was not drawn to scale. Redrawing the figure to scale may help convince you that the areas are equal.

When the square of $2m$ is multiplied by 2, the result is g.

$$m > 0$$

14.

$\dfrac{g}{4m}$	m

Choice **(A)** is correct. The problem states that $(2m)^2 \times 2 = g$, or $8m^2 = g$. To determine the value of $\frac{g}{4m}$, divide both sides of the equation by $4m$ to get $2m = \frac{g}{4m}$. So the value in Column A is $2m$. Since $m > 0$, $2m > m$.

p and *r* are different prime numbers.

15.

The number of positive integer divisors of p^3	The number of positive integer divisors of *pr*

Choice **(C)** is correct. In Column A, the positive integer p^3 can be written as $p \times p \times p$. Since *p* is a prime number, the only positive integer divisors of p^3 are $1, p, p^2$, and p^3 itself, thus p^3 has 4 positive divisors. In Column B, the positive integer *pr* is the product of two different prime numbers *p* and *r*. The positive divisors of *pr* are $1, p, r$, and *pr* itself, thus *pr* also has 4 positive divisors. The quantity in Column A is equal to the quantity in Column B.

16. A certain car's gasoline tank holds 20 gallons when full. The tank is $\frac{3}{4}$ full. At \$1.20 a gallon, how many dollars worth of gasoline must be purchased to fill the remainder of the tank? (Disregard the \$ sign when gridding your answer.)

The correct answer is **\$6.00**. Since the 20-gallon tank is $\frac{3}{4}$ full, multiply $20 \times \frac{3}{4}$ to determine that the tank currently contains 15 gallons of gasoline. Therefore, 5 gallons of gasoline are needed to fill the rest of the car's tank. To determine the number of dollars needed, multiply $\$1.20 \times 5 = \$6.00$. You can enter 6.00 or 6 in the grid.

17. If $\left(3 \times 10^3\right) + \left(2 \times 10^2\right) = a \times 10^3$, what is the value of *a* ?

The correct answer is **3.2** or **16/5**. The equation can be rewritten as $\left(3 \times 10 \times 10^2\right) + \left(2 \times 10^2\right) = a \times 10 \times 10^2$. Dividing both sides of the equation by 10^2 gives $30 + 2 = 10a$. Since $10a = 32$, it follows that $a = 3.2$. The answer can be entered in its decimal form of 3.2 or as the fraction 16/5. The fraction 32/10 cannot be entered in the grid because it contains five symbols and there is only room for four.

18. If $2x + y = 14$ and $4x + y = 20$, what is the value of $3x + y$?

The correct answer is **17**. Add the equations $2x + y = 14$ and $4x + y = 20$.
$14 + 20 = \left(2x + y\right) + \left(4x + y\right) = 6x + 2y = 2\left(3x + y\right)$.
From this it follows that $2\left(3x + y\right) = 34$ and that $\left(3x + y\right) = 17$. If you had noticed that $3x + y$ is the average of $2x + y$ and $4x + y$, you could have taken the average of their values; that is, $\frac{14 + 20}{2} = 17$.

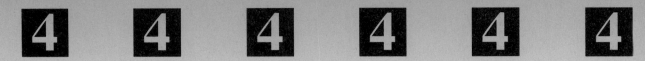

19. What is the number that satisfies the following three conditions?

- It is an integer greater than 999 and less than 1,234.
- The sum of its digits is 14.
- Its tens and units digits are the same

The correct answer is **1166**. Consider each of the three conditions separately to see how you can narrow the set of possible numbers.
- The first condition tells you that the number is a four-digit number of the form $1ABC$, where A is 0, 1, or 2, and B and C are two digits, not necessarily different.
- From the second condition, you know that $14 = 1 + A + B + C$, or $13 = A + B + C$.
- The tens and the units digits of the number are the same, so $B = C$. Substituting, you now have $13 = A + 2B$.

Since 13 is odd and $2B$ is even, A must be odd. Since A is 0, 1, or 2, the only possible value for A is 1. Substituting 1 for A gives $13 = 1 + 2B$. Solving for B, you obtain $B = 6$, and since $B = C$, you have $C = 6$, as well. The number $1ABC$ is 1166. Check that 1166 satisfies all three conditions.

You can also try numbers and solve the problem arithmetically rather than algebraically. The tens and units digits must be less than 7; otherwise, the sum of the digits in the four-digit number would be greater than 14. Knowing that the first digit is 1 and that the last two digits are each less than 7 allows you to narrow in on the correct answer by trial and error. That is, you could look at numbers of the form 1_66, 1_55, etc.

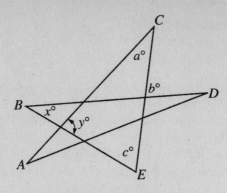

Note: Figure not drawn to scale.

20. In the figure above, AC, CE, EB, BD, and DA are line segments. If $a = 40$, $b = 70$, and $c = 50$, what is the value of $x + y$?

The correct answer is **150**. This problem can be solved by applying two geometric principles.
    (1)   The sum of the measures of the angles of a triangle is 180°.
    (2)   Vertical angles have the same measure.

Label the vertex of the angle marked $b°$ with a letter; for example, F, as shown below.

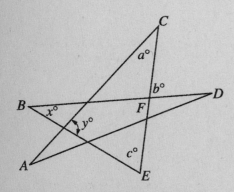

Note: Figure not drawn to scale.

Using principle (2) above, two of the vertical angles at F have a measure of $b°$ or 70°. Now $\angle E$, $\angle B$, and $\angle BFE$ are the three angles of a triangle. Because of principle (1) above and the fact that $c = 50$, you know that $50° + x° + 70° = 180°$. Solving for x, $x = 60$. Also because of principle (1), $y° + a° + c° = 180°$ or $y + 40 + 50 = 180$ and $y = 90$. Therefore, $x + y = 60 + 90 = 150$.

21. For all integers x, let $\boxed{x}$ be defined as follows:

$$\boxed{x} = \frac{x}{2} \text{ if } x \text{ is even.}$$

$$\boxed{x} = x^2 \text{ if } x \text{ is odd.}$$

If $\boxed{2} + \boxed{3} = y$, what is the value of y^3?

The correct answer is **1000**. Since 2 is even, $\boxed{2} = \frac{2}{2} = 1$. Since 3 is odd, $\boxed{3} = 3^2 = 9$. Therefore, $y = 10$ and $y^3 = 1000$.

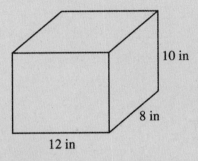

10 in

8 in

12 in

22. A solid block of wood with dimensions as shown in the figure above is to be painted on all of its faces. What is the total area (in square inches) to be painted?

The correct answer is **592** square inches. The total surface area of a block is equal to the sum of the areas of its six faces. The block has two faces that are 12 in. by 8 in., two faces that are 12 in. by 10 in., and two faces that are 8 in. by 10 in. Alternatively, if the three dimensions of the block are l, w, and h, the total surface area is given by the formula $2lw + 2lh + 2wh$. In this case, $l = 12$, $w = 8$, and $h = 10$. Factoring out the 2, you have $2(12 \text{ in.} \times 8 \text{ in.} + 12 \text{ in.} \times 10 \text{ in.} + 8 \text{ in.} \times 10 \text{ in.})$, which equals $2(96 \text{ sq. in.} + 120 \text{ sq. in.} + 80 \text{ sq. in.})$ or 2×296 sq. in. or 592 sq. in.

23. Hakim and Chris began running a 50-yard race at the same time. When Hakim finished the race, Chris was 4 yards behind him. If Hakim ran the race in 7 seconds, what was the difference in their rates in yards per second for those 7 seconds?

The correct answer is $\frac{4}{7}$ or **.571**. In the problem, distance is measured in yards, time is measured in seconds, so the rates will be in yards per second. Use the formula: distance = rate × time, which can be rewritten: rate = $\frac{\text{distance}}{\text{time}}$. Since Hakim ran 50 yards in 7 seconds, his average rate was $\frac{50}{7}$ yards per second. Since Chris ran 46 (which is $50 - 4$) yards in the same time, his average rate was $\frac{46}{7}$ yards per second. Therefore, the difference between Hakim's rate and Chris's rate for these 7 seconds is $\frac{50}{7} - \frac{46}{7} = \frac{4}{7}$ yards per second. You can grid this answer as $\frac{4}{7}$ or as its decimal approximation .571.

24. What is one possible value for the slope of a line passing through point $(-1,1)$ and passing <u>between</u> points $(1,3)$ and $(2,3)$ but not containing either of them?

The correct answer is any number m such that $\frac{2}{3} < m < 1$. The figure shows the position of the three given points (labeled P, Q, and R) in the xy-plane.

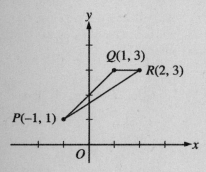

Point Z is located somewhere along segment QR.

For a single quick solution, choose a pair of possible coordinates for Z, say $(1.5, 3)$. The slope of the line that passes

through this chosen point and the point $P(-1,1)$ is given by the equation $\text{slope} = \dfrac{\text{change in } y}{\text{change in } x} = \dfrac{3-1}{1.5-(-1)} = \dfrac{2}{2.5} = \dfrac{20}{25} = \dfrac{4}{5}$.

You can grid $\frac{4}{5}$ or .8 as a possible answer to the question.

To find all possible answers, notice that no matter where Z is located along QR, segment PZ will always be steeper than

segment PR, but not as steep as segment PQ. The slope of PR is $\dfrac{3-1}{2-(-1)} = \dfrac{2}{3}$ and the slope of PQ is $\dfrac{3-1}{1-(-1)} = 1$. Hence,

any number between $\frac{2}{3}$ and 1 is a possible answer to the question.

25. If the average (arithmetic mean) of x, $2x-8$, $2x+2$, $3x-1$, and $4x+1$ is 6, what is the value of the mode of these numbers?

The correct answer is **8**. The given information can be written as the equation $\dfrac{x+2x-8+2x+2+3x-1+4x+1}{5} = 6$. This

can be simplified to $x+2x-8+2x+2+3x-1+4x+1 = 30$ or $12x-6 = 30$. Solving this, you get $12x = 36$ or $x = 3$.
Once you know that x is 3, you can substitute 3 for x and find the five original numbers. $x = 3$,
$2x-8 = -2$, $2x+2 = 8$, $3x-1 = 8$, $4x+1 = 13$. The mode, which is the number that occurs most frequently in the list,
is 8.

1. Mammals of temperate zones often give birth in the spring, thereby------- their offspring to ------- the season's abundant food.

    (A) subjecting . . subsist on
    (B) encouraging . . compete for
    (C) tempting . . abstain from
    (D) forcing . . forage for
    (E) enabling . . benefit from

Choice **(E)** is correct. By giving birth in the spring, mammals of temperate zones are *enabling* or making it possible for their offspring to *benefit from* the abundant food supply available in that season.

Choice (A) is incorrect. To *subject* someone to something is to cause him or her to endure something unpleasant or difficult to deal with. To *subsist* on something is to acquire the necessities of life from it. In this case, mammals of the temperate zones help their offspring to avoid having to deal with difficult conditions by giving birth to them in the spring, when food is plentiful. While *subsist on* fits the context, *subjecting* runs contrary to the sense of the sentence.

2. While the dome of the nineteenth-century city hall once------- the city's skyline, a much taller new office building now------- the old landmark.

    (A) overshadowed . . enhances
    (B) dominated . . dwarfs
    (C) punctuated . . resembles
    (D) cluttered . . destroys
    (E) beautified . . uplifts

Choice **(B)** is correct. To *dwarf* something is to make it appear relatively quite small. A new office building is said to be much taller than a nineteenth century structure; it seems reasonable, then, that the new building *dwarfs* the old landmark, which *dominated* the city's skyline before the construction of its towering rival.

Choice (A) is incorrect. Although it seems implausible for a building to overshadow a city's entire skyline, *overshadowed* could make sense in this sentence. *Enhances*, however, does not. The new and much taller office building does not *enhance* or improve the old landmark in any way. If anything, the new building diminishes the old one.

3. Ancient cloth makers probably could not twist flax fibers until they had dipped the fibers into water to make them -------.

    (A) solvent
    (B) supple
    (C) nonporous
    (D) immutable
    (E) invisible

Choice **(B)** is correct. *Supple* means capable of being bent or shaped; in order to be able to twist flax fibers, ancient cloth makers first had to dip the fibers in water to make them *supple*.

Choice (A) is incorrect. *Solvent* means capable of dissolving or dissolving in another substance. Flax fibers cannot be made *solvent*, but even if they could be they would not be any easier to twist, especially if they have dissolved.

4. In an effort to ------- people's physical discomforts, modern medicine sometimes wrongly treats the body's defense mechanisms as ------- and in need of corrective intervention.

    (A) cure . . complex
    (B) prescribe . . symptomatic
    (C) diagnose . . suppressive
    (D) relieve . . defective
    (E) analyze . . medicinal

Choice **(D)** is correct. While the first terms of other choices seem to make sense, the second terms do not result in a sensible statement. In an effort to *relieve* discomfort, medical science wrongly treats the body's defense mechanisms as needing corrective intervention; the word *defective* most directly conveys the sense of needing corrective intervention.

Choice (C) is incorrect. To *diagnose* a person is to identify the nature of his or her ailment. It is unlikely that modern medicine would treat a person's bodily mechanisms as needing corrective intervention in order to *diagnose* that person's discomforts. *Suppressive* means tending to inhibit or subdue. The word is ambiguous when inserted in the sentence: the bodily mechanisms are *suppressive* of what? Since neither word fits the logic of the sentence, this is not a good choice.

5. *Crazy Love*, by Elías Miguel Muñoz, is an ------- novel: it takes the form of a series of letters.

    (A) archetypal
    (B) epistolary
    (C) inauspicious
    (D) inconspicuous
    (E) illusory

Choice **(B)** is correct. *Epistolary* means carried on through the means of letters; *Crazy Love*, which takes the form of a series of letters, can be characterized as an *epistolary* novel.

Choice (A) is incorrect. To characterize something as *archetypal* is to suggest that it is an ideal example or an original model of its type. Since nothing in the sentence suggests that novels are typically written as a series of letters, *Crazy Love* is most likely not an *archetypal* novel.

6. The meal had ------- effect on the famished travelers: their energy was restored almost instantly.

    (A) a tonic
    (B) a cloying
    (C) an indefinite
    (D) a debilitating
    (E) an intemperate

Choice **(A)** is correct. *Tonic* means tending to refresh or invigorate. If the meal restored the travelers' energy almost immediately, then it had a *tonic* effect—it made them feel refreshed and invigorated.

Choice (C) is incorrect. The meal is said to have restored the travelers' energy. It had a clear and positive effect, not an *indefinite* one, which would have been vague and uncertain.

7. While cynics may ------- the goal of international disarmament as utopian, others believe that laughing
    contemptuously at idealism leads nowhere.

    (A) exalt
    (B) confirm
    (C) renew
    (D) deride
    (E) defend

Choice **(D)** is correct. To *deride* something is to laugh contemptuously at it. Cynics, people who believe that self-interest, rather than noble sentiment, underlies human behavior, might well *deride* international disarmament as a utopian, or naively idealistic, goal. Others, however, believe that to ridicule idealism is to accomplish nothing.

Choice (E) is incorrect. The second half of the sentence implies that cynics are "laughing contemptuously at idealism," something they are not doing if they are "*defending* the goal of international disarmament."

8. Although his memoirs contained scathing criticisms of his opponents, the politician ------- vindictiveness as his motive.

    (A) disavowed
    (B) claimed
    (C) disparaged
    (D) substantiated
    (E) evaluated

Choice **(A)** is correct. To *disavow* something is to refuse to acknowledge it, or to repudiate it. The politician's memoirs contained scathing criticisms of his opponents, which might indicate that he was motivated by "vindictiveness," the desire for revenge. The word "Although" suggests that the politician distanced himself from the implication that he was motivated by the need for revenge—he *disavowed* vindictiveness.

Choice (B) is incorrect. The word *claimed* contradicts the logic of the sentence because "Although" suggests that the politician denied that vindictiveness was his motive.

9. Even in her most casual conversation, one detects the impulse to -------, to impart knowledge systematically to her listener.

    (A) mystify
    (B) instruct
    (C) insinuate
    (D) embellish
    (E) meditate

Choice **(B)** is correct. The parallel structure of the second half of the sentence suggests that what follows the comma restates in expanded form the verb to be inserted in the blank. Since to *instruct* is to "impart knowledge systematically," this word makes the most sense in this sentence.

Choice (C) is incorrect. To *insinuate* is to convey a notion in an indirect, sometimes stealthy or deceptive, manner. When one *insinuates* one does not "impart knowledge systematically."

10. Ms. Turner was an ------- opponent, one who never swerved from her purpose and would never compromise or yield.

    (A) inexorable
    (B) ambivalent
    (C) eloquent
    (D) impassive
    (E) obstreperous

Choice **(A)** is correct. Ms. Turner is described as a person who never swerved from her purpose and who would never compromise or yield. Since *inexorable* means not open to persuasion, or inflexible, Ms. Turner seems the very definition of an *inexorable* opponent.

Choice (D) is incorrect. Ms. Turner cannot be described as an *impassive* opponent: someone *impassive* is apathetic, showing little or no emotion. Ms. Turner, however, is purposeful, uncompromising, and fully committed to her cause.

11. MAP : NAVIGATE ::

    (A) manuscript : submit
    (B) license : revoke
    (C) writing : erase
    (D) blueprint : build
    (E) receipt : pay

Choice **(D)** is correct. A MAP is a document that guides someone who is going to NAVIGATE. A *blueprint* is a document that displays an architect's plans for constructing something. A MAP guides someone who is going to NAVIGATE, just as a *blueprint* guides someone who is going to *build*.

Choice (A) is incorrect. A *manuscript* is a document that someone has written or typed, often for publication. To *submit* a *manuscript* means to present it for consideration or review. A *manuscript* does not help someone who needs to *submit*.

12. SKULL : HEAD ::

    (A) heart : organ
    (B) finger : hand
    (C) skeleton : body
    (D) elbow : joint
    (E) scalp : hair

Choice **(C)** is correct. The SKULL is the bony inner part of a person's HEAD, just as the *skeleton* is the bony inner part of a person's *body*.

Choice (B) is incorrect. A *finger* is part of a person's *hand*, but it is not the bony part inside of the *hand*.

13. ACCOMPLICE : CRIME ::

    (A)   inmate : prison
    (B)   detective : clue
    (C)   employer : work
    (D)   salesperson : store
    (E)   partner : business

Choice **(E)** is correct. An ACCOMPLICE is a person who associates with another person in doing something wrong or illegal. A *partner* is a person who associates with another person, often as a joint principal in a *business*. An ACCOMPLICE along with another person is responsible for a CRIME, just as a *partner* along with another person is responsible for a *business*.

Choice (C) is incorrect. An *employer* hires people who perform the *work* of business. The *employer* does not, by definition, share responsibility for organizing and directing the *work* with another person.

14. BARRICADE : ACCESS ::

    (A)   heal : illness
    (B)   demand : due
    (C)   bind : movement
    (D)   complete : task
    (E)   chat : conversation

Choice **(C)** is correct. To BARRICADE something is to block it off so that there is no ACCESS. To *bind* something is to tie it so that it can't be moved. To BARRICADE prevents ACCESS, just as to *bind* prevents *movement*.

Choice (A) is incorrect. To *heal* someone is to restore him or her to health. To *heal* someone of an *illness* involves ending the *illness*, not preventing it.

15. ENSEMBLE : DANCER ::

    (A)   clique : outsider
    (B)   band : musician
    (C)   gymnasium : athlete
    (D)   museum : curator
    (E)   audience : performer

Choice **(B)** is correct. When ENSEMBLE refers to people, it means a group that performs together. A DANCER performs as part of an ENSEMBLE, just as a *musician* performs as part of a *band*.

Choice (E) is incorrect. A *performer* is not part of an *audience*, but instead presents a *performance* for an *audience*.

16. CONSIDER : CONTEMPLATE ::

    (A)   smile : greet
    (B)   write : compose
    (C)   complain : bicker
    (D)   examine : scrutinize
    (E)   ignore : notice

Choice **(D)** is correct. To CONSIDER something is to think about it and to CONTEMPLATE something is to CONSIDER it carefully and attentively. To *scrutinize* something is to *examine* it in detail. To CONTEMPLATE something is to CONSIDER it carefully, just as to *scrutinize* something is to *examine* it carefully.

Choice (C) is incorrect. To *bicker* is to argue in a petty way. An unpleasant situation might make a person *complain* as well as *bicker*, but to *bicker* does not mean to *complain* carefully.

17. CONGEAL : SOLID ::

    (A)   heat : fire
    (B)   breathe : air
    (C)   immunize : disease
    (D)   melt : liquid
    (E)   push : resistance

Choice **(D)** is correct. To CONGEAL means to become a SOLID. Something that CONGEALs turns into a SOLID, just as something that *melts* turns into a *liquid*.

Choice (A) is incorrect. Although *fire* can be used to *heat* something, to *heat* something does not make it become a *fire*.

18. SHEAR : WOOL ::

    (A)   reap : wheat
    (B)   whittle : wood
    (C)   sweep : broom
    (D)   prune : tree
    (E)   rake : leaves

Choice **(A)** is correct. To SHEAR means to cut WOOL from a sheep. To *reap* means to cut grain in order to harvest it. To SHEAR is to cut WOOL, just as to *reap* is to cut *wheat*.

Choice (D) is incorrect. To *prune* means to trim or shape something by cutting away parts of it. To *prune* a *tree* is to trim or shape the *tree*, not to remove it altogether, as SHEARING does with WOOL.

19. EPILOGUE : BOOK ::

    (A)   sequel : movie
    (B)   conclusion : title
    (C)   tiff : quarrel
    (D)   intermission : play
    (E)   finale : symphony

Choice **(E)** is correct. An EPILOGUE is a section that appears at the end of a BOOK. The *finale* is the last part of a long musical composition, such as a *symphony*. An EPILOGUE comes at the end of a BOOK, just as a *finale* comes at the end of a *symphony*.

Choice (A) is incorrect. A *sequel* continues a story begun in an earlier book or *movie*. A *sequel* does not appear at the end of a *movie*, but is a *movie* of its own that follows the preceding *movie*.

20. GLUTTON : MODERATION ::

    (A)   thief : larceny
    (B)   peer : nobility
    (C)   scoundrel : virtue
    (D)   gambler : luck
    (E)   benefactor : gift

Choice **(C)** is correct. A GLUTTON eats large quantities of food in a greedy way. A person who shows MODERATION is one who avoids extreme or excessive behavior. A GLUTTON lacks MODERATION, just as a *scoundrel* lacks *virtue*.

Choice (D) is incorrect. A *gambler* is a person who plays games of chance, where success is determined by a person's *luck* or good fortune. A *gambler* is not by definition someone who lacks *luck*, but rather a person who needs good *luck* in order to win.

21. AFFECTATION : BEHAVIOR ::

    (A)   speech : topic
    (B)   tension : violence
    (C)   façade : appearance
    (D)   buffoonery : action
    (E)   pretense : honesty

Choice **(C)** is correct. AFFECTATION means BEHAVIOR that is artificial, that presents an inaccurate impression of a person's nature or feelings. *Façade* indicates a deliberately misleading *appearance*, like an impressive front attached to an otherwise small and unremarkable building. An AFFECTATION is a deliberately misleading BEHAVIOR, just as a *façade* is a deliberately misleading *appearance*.

Choice (D) is incorrect. *Buffoonery* means playful or foolish behavior. *Buffoonery* is not a deliberately misleading type of *action*.

22. EXHORTATION : URGE ::

    (A)   division : unite
    (B)   agreement : dissent
    (C)   eulogy : praise
    (D)   travesty : reproduce
    (E)   charity : donate

Choice **(C)** is correct. An EXHORTATION is a speech that URGEs the audience strongly to do something. A *eulogy* is a speech that *praises* someone, usually at a funeral. The purpose of an EXHORTATION is to URGE, just as the purpose of a *eulogy* is to *praise*.

Choice (E) is incorrect. A *charity* is an organization dedicated to helping others. Funding for a *charity* often depends on money that people *donate*. The words do not fit the relationship—a *charity* is not a speech that *donates* its listeners.

23. COOPERATION : COLLUSION ::

   (A)   evidence : proof
   (B)   achievement : reward
   (C)   damage : compensation
   (D)   imitation : forgery
   (E)   emotion : ecstasy

Choice **(D)** is correct. COLLUSION means secret agreement to take part in a deceitful and often illegal activity. People guilty of COLLUSION work together on an illegal activity. *Forgery* involves making an *imitation* of something for an illegal purpose. COLLUSION is a form of COOPERATION for illegal purposes, just as *forgery* is a form of *imitation* for illegal purposes.

Choice (B) is incorrect. A *reward* may be given to someone in recognition of a special *achievement*. A *reward* is not a form of *achievement* for illegal purposes.

24. The passage as a whole can best be described as an expression of

   (A)   amusement at the behavior of muskrats
   (B)   regret at the impact of humans on the lake
   (C)   scorn for the people who use the lake
   (D)   optimism about the future of the lake
   (E)   irritation at the modern obsession with speed

Choice **(B)** is correct. This choice is the best response because it is supported by statements made in the passage, particularly in the first paragraph. The author begins with the statement that he recently visited a lake "that has been preempted and civilized by human beings." His use of the word "preempted" (meaning seized upon to the exclusion of others) is the first indication that he views humans as having a negative impact on the lake. He follows this statement with a description of the "reckless" young people who dominate the lake with their "high-speed motorboats." Later, the author reinforces his point by making reference to the "washed-in beer cans" on the shores of the lake and by repeating the word "preempted" in his grim description of the muskrat "caught between a vanishing forest and a deep lake preempted by unpredictable machines full of chopping blades" (lines 53–54).

Choice (C) is incorrect. Although the author does express resentment toward young people who drive motorboats with "reckless abandon," and perhaps scorn for the people who discarded the "washed-in beer cans," the passage as a whole is less angry than it is regretful. The author primarily focuses on the predicament of the muskrat and the inevitable disappearance of "a natural world." In the last paragraph, the author describes the vanishing muskrat wistfully: "As he vanished in an oncoming wave, there went with him a natural world, distinct from the world of young people and motorboats …. It was a world of sunlight he had taken down into the water weeds" (lines 71–75).

25. Lines 3–9 indicate that the word "civilized" (line 2) is being used

   (A)   cautiously
   (B)   sarcastically
   (C)   humorously
   (D)   hopefully
   (E)   wistfully

Choice **(B)** is correct. Lines 3–9 describe motorboats being driven with "reckless abandon," the shores echoing "to the roar of powerful motors and the delighted screams of young people with uncounted horsepower surging under their hands." One definition of "civilized" behavior is behavior that seems restrained or refined. The contrast between this meaning of the word and the behavior exhibited by the young people indicates that "civilized" is being used in a *sarcastic* way.

Choice (E) is incorrect. Although the author may seem wistful, or full of yearning, about the disappearance of the "natural" lake, lines 3–9 do not express that *wistfulness*. These lines describe the "reckless" behavior of the young people driving the motorboats.

26. The underlying sentiment in the sentence beginning "If I had" (lines 9–12) is the author's

(A) nostalgia for experiences that are no longer possible
(B) grudging admiration for young people
(C) regret for something he had failed to do
(D) amusement at his own foolishness
(E) feeling of moral paralysis

Choice **(A)** is correct. In lines 9–12, the author indicates that a desire to swim or canoe "in the older ways of the forest that once lay about this region" would be foolish since it's no longer safe to swim or canoe in most of the lake. The author's reference to "older" ways and to the forest that "once" surrounded the region reinforces the feeling of *nostalgia* for something that no longer exists.

Choice (E) is incorrect. Although the author may feel frustrated by the realization that he cannot do the things he may want to do, nothing suggests that he is experiencing moral paralysis, the inability to take a moral position. The author makes it clear in lines 53–54 that he disapproves of the "unpredictable machines full of chopping blades."

27. In lines 12–15, the author suggests that the young people are

(A) competitive
(B) violent
(C) self-absorbed
(D) rebellious
(E) uninformed

Choice **(C)** is correct. In lines 12–15, the author imagines himself endangered by "young people whose eyes were always immutably fixed on the far horizons of space, or on the dials which indicated the speed of their passing." His use of the word "gaily" suggests that the young people were oblivious to the consequences of their actions. His description of their "immutably fixed" eyes also indicates how intently they were *self-absorbed*.

Choice (A) is incorrect. Although the references to the speed of the motorboats may suggest that the young people are competitive, the author's description of the young people's "immutably fixed" eyes emphasizes the self-absorption of the young people rather than their *competitiveness*.

28. In line 27, "broke" most nearly means

(A) destroyed
(B) surpassed
(C) weakened
(D) pierced
(E) tamed

Choice **(D)** is correct. In lines 26–27, the author describes the muskrat coming to the surface of the lake: "A furry nose with gray whiskers broke the surface." He goes on to describe how "Below the whiskers, green water foliage trailed out in an inverted V as long as his body." Although the word "break" has many meanings, the meaning that makes most sense here is that of rupturing or penetrating. The muskrat's head penetrated the surface of the water and the rest of his body remained at or just below the surface. Since *pierced* means making a hole in or penetrating something, it is reasonable to conclude that "broke" most nearly means *pierced* in this context.

Choice (B) is incorrect. Although "broken" can mean *surpassed* in some contexts, such as when a record is "broken," this is not what it means here. The surface of the water has not been *surpassed*, or exceeded.

29. In the sentence beginning in line 33 ("He was young . . . Garden of Eden"), the author suggests that

    (A)   in this lake, few muskrats have the chance to reach maturity
    (B)   an older, wiser muskrat would have learned to fear people
    (C)   the muskrat was only one of several types of animals living in the lake
    (D)   at one time the lake had been home to a variety of animals
    (E)   some parts of the lake had remained unchanged for centuries

Choice **(B)** is correct. In lines 33–37, the muskrat is described as "young" and "laboring under an illusion" that animals and people are living together in an idyllic world. It can be inferred from these lines that if the muskrat were older, he would recognize that animals and people were no longer "living in the Garden of Eden." Later, the author reinforces this idea by describing how the muskrat responds when a pebble is tossed at his feet: "He made almost as if to take the pebble up into his forepaws. Then a thought seemed to cross his mind: perhaps after all this was not Eden. His nose twitched carefully; he edged toward the water" (lines 57–60). Clearly, with more experience, and the "wisdom" experience brings, the muskrat does in fact learn to "fear people."

Choice (D) is incorrect. While the author does note in lines 21–22 that the muskrat was "the first sign of life I had seen in this lake," he does not indicate that the lake was once *home to a variety of animals*. In lines 33–37, he focuses on the muskrat's apparent view of the relationship between animals and people, not on the numbers or types of animals that may have inhabited the lake at one time.

30. In line 35, "laboring under" most nearly means

    (A)   moving with great effort
    (B)   being exploited by
    (C)   striving to achieve
    (D)   working for
    (E)   suffering from

Choice **(E)** is correct. In line 35, the author writes that the muskrat was "laboring under an illusion . . . that . . . animals and people were still living in the Garden of Eden." This illusion leads the muskrat to give the author a "friendly glance" rather than recognize how dangerous human beings are. The author suggests that the muskrat holds an incorrect belief that may be dangerous and cause him to suffer. Therefore, it makes sense to say that "laboring under" most nearly means *suffering from* in this context.

Choice (B) is incorrect. It is clear from the author's discussion that he views the muskrat's "illusion" as being dangerous for the muskrat. However, the author does not suggest at any point that this "illusion" is being used to exploit, or to take advantage of, the muskrat. In fact, the author states that the muskrat is "laboring under an illusion of *his own*," not an illusion imposed by anyone else.

31. The author probably "shuddered" (line 41) because

    (A)   he was afraid of the muskrat
    (B)   he envisioned what could happen to the muskrat
    (C)   he was sitting in shade under the boat dock
    (D)   the behavior of the young people in the motorboats frightened him
    (E)   he wondered what else could happen to undermine the ecology of the lake

Choice **(B)** is correct. In the lines that follow the statement "I shuddered," the author recalls how his neighbor described "how he had killed a muskrat in the garden." The author is concerned about the dangers facing muskrats; he mentions shuddering immediately before his recollection because he is imagining what might happen to this particular muskrat.

Choice (E) is incorrect. Nothing in the passage indicates that the author is concerned about the *ecology of the lake* at this moment. His description of the neighbor's story in lines 41–45 shows that he is primarily concerned about the muskrat's safety.

32. The phrase "dared to" in line 45 emphasizes the author's belief that

(A) the muskrat was dangerous
(B) the muskrat was insolent
(C) humans will eventually destroy all life in the lake
(D) the neighbor's behavior was uncalled for
(E) the author felt intimidated by his neighbor

Choice **(D)** is correct. In lines 42–45, the author recalls his neighbor's description of how "he had killed a muskrat in the garden." The author offers his own view of the event when he suggests that his neighbor killed the muskrat "because the creature had dared to nibble his petunias." Since nibbling is not a "daring" or bold act, the author's description appears to be ironic, saying the opposite of what the author means. The author's use of the phrase "dared to," then, conveys his belief that the muskrat was not a serious threat and that the neighbor's response was *uncalled for*.

Choice (B) is incorrect. While the phrase "dared to" suggests that the muskrat did something bold or even *insolent*, what follows—"to nibble his petunias"—is not an example of bold or *insolent* behavior. The entire statement ("dared to . . . petunias") offers an ironic view of the muskrat's actions.

33. The quotation in lines 58–62 primarily serves as a warning about the

(A) threat from the author
(B) behavior of humans in general
(C) predatory nature of many wild animals
(D) inevitable destruction of the natural world
(E) callousness of the young people in the motorboats

Choice **(B)** is correct. In lines 59–62, the author warns the muskrat that he is in danger: "You are in the wrong universe and must not make this mistake again. I am really a very terrible and cunning beast. I can throw stones." In describing himself as a "cunning beast" who "can throw stones," the author implies that the danger the muskrat faces is not only from him but from humans in general, since humans use weapons. Thus, it makes sense to say that the author is warning the muskrat about the *behavior of humans in general*.

Choice (D) is incorrect. Although the author observes in lines 46–47 that on the lake shore "a war existed and would go on until nothing remained but human beings," he does not discuss the *inevitable destruction of the natural world* in his warning to the muskrat. In lines 59–62, the author emphasizes the immediate danger facing the muskrat: the "terrible and cunning beast" who can "throw stones."

34. Which of the following best describes the author's action in lines 62–63 ("With this . . . at his feet") as compared to his words in lines 58–62?

(A) His action exaggerates his words.
(B) His action is more admirable than his words.
(C) His action reveals a hidden dimension to his words.
(D) His action parallels the severity of his words.
(E) His action is much less emphatic than his words.

Choice **(E)** is correct. In lines 58–62, the author informs the muskrat that he, as a human, is "a very terrible and cunning beast" who can "throw stones." We might expect the author to follow this threat with a demonstration of truly menacing behavior, but the author instead "dropped a little pebble" at the muskrat's feet. This is so non-threatening that the muskrat initially responds by considering taking the pebble "up into his forepaws," as though the pebble were a gift. The author's action is much milder and *less emphatic* than his threatening words predicted.

Choice (D) is incorrect. The author's behavior is not consistent with his threats of danger. In fact, dropping "a little pebble at his feet" does not parallel the severity of the author's words.

35. In the last sentence (lines 75–76), the author implies that

(A) **he himself does not belong to the natural world**
(B) his fears have been unfounded
(C) his behavior has been unacceptable
(D) humans will eventually learn to behave responsibly toward nature
(E) there is no future for the young muskrat

Choice **(A)** is correct. In lines 71–73, the author describes the muskrat vanishing in a wave, taking with him "a natural world, distinct from the world of young people and motorboats." He then indicates that this world "hovered there, waiting for my disappearance." These references show that the author feels he *does not belong to the natural world*. In addition, the final lines imply that the natural world, and the muskrat that is a part of it, cannot thrive until the author leaves.

Choice (E) is incorrect. Although the author points out in lines 46–47 that "a war existed" on the shore of this lake and that "it would go on until nothing remained but human beings," he does not make this same point in the last sentence of the passage. In lines 75–76, the author writes that the "world of sunlight" is "waiting for [the author's] disappearance." The idea that the natural world is waiting for the author to leave does not mean that the muskrat's future is in question. Rather, it implies that the muskrat can thrive in the natural world as long as he keeps his distance from human beings.

1. If $x = 2y$ and $y = \dfrac{10}{z}$, what is the value of x when $z = 4$?

   (A) $\dfrac{5}{4}$

   (B) $\dfrac{5}{2}$

   (C) 5

   (D) 8

   (E) 20

Choice **(C)** is correct. If $x = 2y$, $y = \dfrac{10}{z}$, and $z = 4$, then $x = 2y = 2\left(\dfrac{10}{4}\right) = \dfrac{10}{2} = 5$.

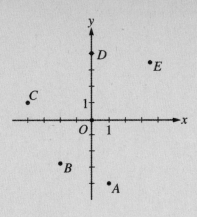

2. In the figure above, which lettered point, other than point O, lies in the interior of a circle with center O and radius 4 ?

(A) A
(B) B
(C) C
(D) D
(E) E

Choice **(B)** is correct. To answer this question, you can sketch the circle centered at O with a radius of 4.

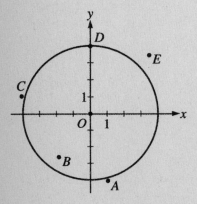

Point D lies on the circle and points C, E, and A lie just outside the circle. The correct answer is B, the only point in the interior of the circle. To assure yourself that point A does indeed lie outside the circle, you can use the distance formula to show that the distance between points O and A is greater than 4. The distance formula is a special application of the Pythagorean Theorem in the coordinate plane. If two points have coordinates (x_1, y_1) and (x_2, y_2), respectively, then the distance beween them is given by the formula $\sqrt{(x_2 - x_1)^2 + (y_2 - y_1)^2}$. For the points $O(0, 0)$ and $A(1, -4)$, the distance is $\sqrt{(1-0)^2 + (-4-0)^2}$ or $\sqrt{1+16}$ or $\sqrt{17}$. Since $\sqrt{17} > 4$, point A is outside the circle. Similarly, the distance between points O and C is also $\sqrt{17}$.

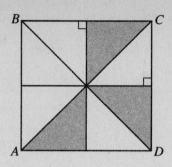

3. In the figure above, *ABCD* is a square. What percent of the square is shaded?

(A) 25%

(B) $33\frac{1}{3}$%

(C) $37\frac{1}{2}$%

(D) 40%

(E) 50%

Choice **(C)** is correct. The two diagonals divide the square into 4 equal regions. Since the line segments that are perpendicular to the sides go through the center of the square, there are 8 equal regions. That is, there are 8 congruent triangles, which have equal areas. Since 3 of them are shaded, $\frac{3}{8}$ or $37\frac{1}{2}$% of the square is shaded.

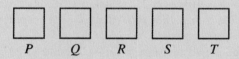

P   Q   R   S   T

4. Each of the boxes above must contain one number from the set {8, 15, 16, 18, 27}. A different number is to be placed in each box so that the following conditions are met.

(1) Box *P* contains an odd number.
(2) Box *Q* contains an even number.
(3) Boxes *R* and *S* each contain a number that is a multiple of 9.
(4) The number in box *P* is less than the number in box *Q*.

What number must be in box *T*?

(A) 8
(B) 15
(C) 16
(D) 18
(E) 27

Choice **(A)** is correct. Considering condition (3) first, 18 and 27 are placed in boxes *R* and *S*. Then, conditions (4), (1), and (2) force 15 and 16 be placed in boxes *P* and *Q*, respectively. This leaves 8 to be placed in box *T*.

Questions 5-6 refer to the following graphs, which show the change in the number and average (arithmetic mean) size of farms in the United States during the years 1940-1990.

UNITED STATES FARMS, 1940–1990

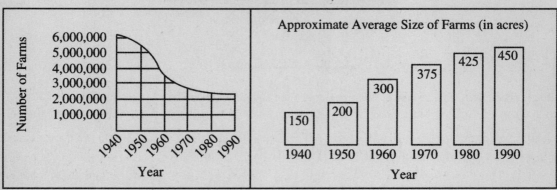

5. Which of the following is NOT a valid conclusion from the information shown in the graphs?

(A) From 1950 to 1960, the number of farms decreased by approximately 2,000,000.
(B) From 1940 to 1990, the number of farms decreased.
(C) From 1940 to 1990, the average size of farms increased each decade.
(D) In 1980, there were about 2,500,000 farms.
(E) From 1950 to 1960, the average size of farms increased by approximately 100%.

Choice **(E)** is correct. Read each choice and decide which one is false.
(A) In 1950 there were approximately 5,500,000 farms and in 1960 there were approximately 3,500,000 farms, a decrease of approximately 2,000,000. This statement is true.
(B) Since the curve in the graph on the left continuously goes down, it shows that the number of farms decreased with each passing year from over 6,000,000 in 1940 to a little over 2,000,000 in 1990. This statement is true.
(C) Since the bars in the bar graph increase in size, they show that for each 10-year period the average size of farms increased. This is a true statement.
(D) In 1980 the number of farms was about halfway between 2,000,000 and 3,000,000, or approximately 2,500,000. This statement is true.
(E) From 1950 to 1960, the average size of farms increased by 100 acres. Since 100 is 50% of 200, this was a 50% increase, not a 100% increase. This statement is **false**.

6. According to the graphs, which of the following is the best estimate of the total acreage of farms in 1950 ?

(A)   200,000
(B)   1,100,000
(C)   5,500,000
(D)   1,100,000,000
(E) 11,000,000,000

Choice (D) is correct. In 1950 there were approximately 5,500,000 farms in the U.S. The average size of each farm was 200 acres. To find the total acreage, multiply the number of farms by the average number of acres per farm.

$$\text{Total Acreage} = \left(5,500,000 \text{ Farms}\right) \times \left(200 \frac{\text{Acres}}{\text{Farm}}\right) = 1,100,000,000 \text{ Acres}$$

52

7. In the exact middle of a certain book, when the page numbers on the facing pages, x and $x+1$, are multiplied together, the product is 210. If all of the pages are numbered in order, how many numbered pages are in the book?

    (A) 24
    (B) 26
    (C) 28
    (D) 32
    (E) 34

Choice **(C)** is correct. Since x is a positive integer such that $x(x+1) = 210$, it is not necessary to solve this quadratic

equation directly. The value of x must be close to $\sqrt{210}$, which is slightly more than 14. Notice that $x = 14$ satisfies the equation, so in the exact middle of the book, the page numbers on the facing pages are 14 and 15. (Alternatively, you can

solve the quadratic equation $x^2 + x - 210 = 0$, or $(x+15)(x-14) = 0$, and $x = 14$.) By definition of the exact middle of a book, there must be as many numbered pages before page 14 as there are after page 15. Since there are 13 numbered pages before page 14, there must be an additional 13 numbered pages after page 15. This makes the total of the numbered pages equal to $15 + 13 = 28$.

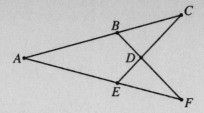

8. Segments *AC*, *AF*, *BF*, and *EC* intersect at the labeled points as shown in the figure above. Define two points as "independent" if they do not lie on the same segment in the figure. Of the labeled points in the figure, how many pairs of independent points are there?

(A) None
(B) One
(C) Two
(D) Three
(E) Four

Choice **(D)** is correct. In order to find two points that are "independent," you must find two points that do not lie on the same segment in the figure. In this table, every combination of points is listed without repetition.

Combination of Points	Lie on Same Segment
A, B	Yes
A, C	Yes
A, D	**No**
A, E	Yes
A, F	Yes
B, C	Yes
B, D	Yes
B, E	**No**
B, F	Yes
C, D	Yes
C, E	Yes
C, F	**No**
D, E	Yes
D, F	Yes
E, F	Yes

According to the chart, the pair of points *A* and *D* are "independent," as are *B* and *E*, and *C* and *F*.

9. If a and b are positive integers, which of the following expressions is equivalent to $\dfrac{\left(3^a\right)^b}{3^a}$?

(A) 1^b

(B) 3^b

(C) 3^{ab-1}

(D) $3^{ab} - 3^a$

(E) $\left(3^a\right)^{b-1}$

Choice **(E)** is correct. Use the rules for exponents to simplify the fraction $\dfrac{\left(3^a\right)^b}{3^a}$. Based on the rules, $\left(3^a\right)^b$ is equivalent to

3^{ab}. The fraction can be written as 3^{ab-a}, which is equivalent to $\left(3^a\right)^{b-1}$.

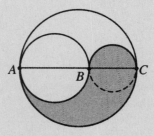

Note: Figure not drawn to scale.

10. AB, BC, and AC are diameters of the three circles shown above. If $BC = 2$ and $AB = 2BC$, what is the area of the shaded region?

(A) 12π

(B) 6π

(C) $\dfrac{9}{2}\pi$

(D) 3π

(E) 2π

Choice **(D)** is correct. The area of the shaded region is equal to the area of the large semicircle minus the area of the medium semicircle, plus the area of the small semicircle. Since BC, the diameter of the small circle, is 2, the radius is 1, so

the small circle has an area of π. Hence, the small semicircle has area $\dfrac{\pi}{2}$. Since the diameter of the medium circle is AB,

and since $AB = 2BC = 4$, the radius of the medium circle is 2. The area of the medium semicircle is $\dfrac{2^2\pi}{2} = 2\pi$. The

diameter of the large circle is $AB + BC$ or $4 + 2$ or 6 and its radius is 3. The area of the large semicircle is $\dfrac{3^2\pi}{2} = \dfrac{9}{2}\pi$. The

area of the shaded region, then, is $\dfrac{9}{2}\pi - 2\pi + \dfrac{\pi}{2} = 3\pi$.

55

1. In the first paragraph of Passage 1, the attitude of the author toward Linnaeus' legacy is one of

    (A) nostalgia
    (B) appreciation
    (C) delight
    (D) bafflement
    (E) resentment

Choice **(B)** is correct. In line 1, the author describes Linnaeus' contribution to natural history as "enormous and essential." The author also refers to Linnaeus' inventions as "innovations" and observes that these innovations "may sound unexciting until one tries to imagine a world without these fundamental tools...." All of these statements communicate the author's *appreciation* for Linnaeus' legacy.

Choice (A) is incorrect. *Nostalgia* refers to a sentimental yearning for some period in the past. Although the author clearly admires Linnaeus' achievements, nothing in the paragraph suggests that the author yearns for a return to Linnaeus' time period. In fact, the author emphasizes the contemporary value of Linnaeus' innovations in noting that one of Linnaeus' innovations is "still used today."

2. The word "case" as it is used in line 10 most nearly means

    (A) example
    (B) lawsuit
    (C) convincing argument
    (D) set of circumstances
    (E) situation under investigation

Choice **(D)** is correct. In lines 7–11, the author attempts to show the significance of Linnaeus' innovations by asking the reader to "imagine a scientific world without these fundamental tools—as was indeed the case with natural history before the Linnaean system." The second half of the sentence makes reference to the field of natural history and what it consisted of before Linnaeus' innovations. The word "case," then, refers to the situation or *set of circumstances* in the field of natural history before Linnaeus' innovations.

Choice (A) is incorrect. The author is discussing the situation or *set of circumstances* in natural history before the Linnaean system, not the *example* of natural history before the Linnaean system.

3. The discussion of "a shell" in lines 26–29 serves primarily to illustrate

    (A) what types of Latin names were commonly used for biological species in Linnaeus' day
    (B) why the Linnaean system of naming was trivial in comparison to another innovation
    (C) why other naturalists initially opposed the Linnaean system of naming
    (D) how the Linnaean system helped naturalists identify previously unknown species
    (E) how the Linnaean system simplified the names of biological species

Choice **(E)** is correct. In lines 22–26, the author states that Linnaeus' "reducing the name of each species to two words" was "an invaluable break with the past." The author then offers the example of the shell, emphasizing the conciseness of its new name: "For instance, a shell with earlier names such as 'Marbled Jamaica Murex with Knotty Twirls (Petiver)' became simply *Strombus gigas* L." The shell illustrates the simplicity of Linnaeus' system of naming.

Choice (A) is incorrect. The author points out that Linnaeus "followed the custom of his time" when he used Latin to name species (lines 21–22), but does not discuss the types of Latin names that were commonly used in Linnaeus' day.

4. As used in line 31, "vital" most nearly means

    (A) animated
    (B) invigorating
    (C) essential
    (D) necessary to maintaining life
    (E) characteristic of living beings

Choice **(C)** is correct. In lines 30–32, the author indicates that while Linnaeus' system of nomenclature may seem "vital," it was a "trivial" invention compared to his "main achievement." "Vital" is used to contrast with "trivial." "Vital," then, in this context, means *essential*, the opposite of "trivial."

Choice (D) is incorrect. While "vital" can, in some contexts, mean *necessary to maintaining life*, this is not what it means here. Linnaeus' system of nomenclature is essential in identifying living organisms; it is not necessary for the maintenance of life.

5. Passage 1 indicates that Linnaeus' classification of the natural kingdom was based on

    (A) the conclusions of previous naturalists
    (B) a conception of nature's order
    (C) the idea that classifying forms the basis of biological inquiry
    (D) close observation of nature's patterns
    (E) a theory about how biological species developed over time

Choice **(B)** is correct. In lines 41–45, the author states that Linnaeus' classifications "reflect an eighteenth-century concept of nature in which all organisms, graded from lower to higher, formed a ladder or 'great chain of being,' with the human species at the summit." The "great chain of being" described here can best be characterized as a *conception of nature's order*.

Choice (C) is incorrect. This choice directly contradicts the author's statement in lines 46–48 of Passage 1: "Linnaeus himself would probably have been the first to admit that classification is only a tool, and not the ultimate purpose, of biological inquiry." In addition, the author argues that Linnaeus' immediate successors were misguided in their tendency "to concern themselves almost exclusively with classification" (lines 51–52).

6. In Passage 2, the author mentions that the garden "is closer to an explosion" (line 72) in order to

    (A) illustrate the impact that Linnaeus' fame had on the town of Uppsala
    (B) emphasize the influence that Linnaeus has had on human thought
    (C) call attention to the profusion of growth in the small garden
    (D) note that the seeds that Linnaeus planted in the garden have grown into large trees
    (E) express concern about the destructive potential of scientific advancement

Choice **(B)** is correct. In lines 73–74, the author characterizes the "explosion" mentioned in the previous line as having "reverberations" that "continue to resonate inside the human brain." The author also describes the garden as "the place where an intellectual seed landed" that has "now grown to a tree that shadows the entire globe" (lines 75–76). These descriptions demonstrate the extent of Linnaeus' impact on human thought.

Choice (E) is incorrect. Although the word "explosion" may indicate a destructive effect, this answer is too sweeping. While the author certainly has reservations about the effect of Linnaeus' work, there is no suggestion about a broader concern about the *destructive potential of scientific advancement*.

7. The author of Passage 2 characterizes "much of science" (line 81) as

    (A) reductive
    (B) innovative
    (C) controversial
    (D) idealistic
    (E) obscure

Choice **(A)** is correct. *Reductive* means oversimplified, such as when complex data or phenomena are reduced to simple terms. In lines 81–84, the author argues that after Linnaeus, "much of science has been devoted to providing specific labels, to explaining specific mechanisms—to sorting masses into individual entities and arranging the entities neatly." This emphasis on labeling and arranging, to the exclusion of other concerns, could accurately be characterized as *reductive*.

Choice **(D)** is incorrect. *Idealistic* means guided by impractical standards of perfection or excellence rather than by practical considerations. In Passage 2, the author indicates that after Linnaeus, "much of science" has concentrated on labeling and arranging things. Nothing in the passage suggests that this approach involves impractical standards of excellence. If anything, this approach would be considered practical.

8. As used in lines 87–88, "apprehending" most nearly means

    (A) seizing
    (B) anticipating
    (C) fearing
    (D) understanding
    (E) doubting

Choice **(D)** is correct. In lines 84–88, the author points out that the "cost of having so successfully itemized and pigeonholed nature . . . is to limit certain possibilities of seeing and apprehending." In the following line, the author provides an example to support this statement: "For example, the modern human thinks that he or she can best understand a tree (or a species of tree) by examining a single tree. But trees are not intended to grow in isolation." The use of the word "understand" indicates that "apprehending," in lines 87–88, means *understanding* something.

Choice **(A)** is incorrect. Although "apprehending" can mean *seizing* in some contexts, such as when a criminal is apprehended, this is not what it means in this context. Nothing in the passage suggests that anyone or anything is being *seized*.

9. The author of Passage 2 suggests that the "scientific view of the external world" (lines 97–98) involves

    (A) perceiving the actual chaos of nature
    (B) recognizing that plants and animals are social creatures
    (C) limiting one's understanding of the world
    (D) appreciating nature only for its usefulness to humans
    (E) performing experiments with potentially destructive results

Choice **(C)** is correct. In lines 80–88, the author of Passage 2 discusses the focus of science since Linnaeus—in particular, the preoccupation with labeling and arranging that has had the effect of limiting "certain possibilities of seeing and apprehending." The author is asserting that the scientific view of the external world limits one's understanding of the world. The author then argues that the external world is a far more complex place than the scientific view acknowledges.

Choice **(A)** is incorrect. This answer may at first seem reasonable since the passage describes the world as "quintessentially 'wild': irrational, uncontrollable, incalculable" (lines 104–105). But the author of Passage 2 argues that science fails to understand this. Lines 85–86 state that science has "successfully itemized and pigeonholed nature," that it has sought to "name" and "explain" it. So science, the author would argue, has actually <u>failed</u> to perceive the *actual chaos of nature*.

10. Which of the following techniques is used in <u>each</u> of the last two sentences of Passage 2 (lines 104–109) ?

    (A) Comparison and contrast
    (B) Personal anecdote
    (C) Elaboration of terms
    (D) Summary of opposing arguments
    (E) Illustration by example

Choice **(C)** is correct. In lines 104–109, the author characterizes the experience of humans in the external world as "quintessentially 'wild': irrational, uncontrollable, incalculable." The author then observes that despite humans' attempts to "'garden' everyday experience, to invent…systems for it," this experience in fact "resembles wild nature, the green chaos of the woods." In both these sentences, the author makes observations (the world is "wild"; humans' attempts to "garden" their experiences) and then elaborates on them by providing additional words or phrases that reinforce the observations.

Choice (E) is incorrect. Although the author may appear to be providing examples to illustrate points in lines 104–109, the words or phrases provided here ("irrational, uncontrollable, incalculable" and "the green chaos of the woods") are not examples of the words they modify, but additional details of those words. They reinforce the original statements; they are not examples of them.

11. The approaches of the two passages to the topic of Linnaeus differ in that only Passage 2 uses

    (A) second-person address to the reader
    (B) several specific examples of Linnaean nomenclature
    (C) an anecdote from the author's personal experience
    (D) references to other authors who have written about Linnaeus
    (E) a comparison between Linnaeus' system and other types of scientific innovations

Choice **(C)** is correct. Passage 2 begins with a first-person anecdote about the author's recent visit to Linnaeus' garden in Uppsala, Sweden. Passage 1 uses the third-person address, providing a more objective and impersonal tone.

Choice (E) is incorrect. Passage 1 makes a comparison between Linnaeus' system and other types of innovations, but the comparison is between Linnaeus' own two innovations: his system of nomenclature and his classification system (lines 30–35). Passage 2 does not discuss any scientific innovations other than Linnaeus'.

12. Both passages emphasize which of the following aspects of Linnaeus' work?

    (A) The extent to which it represented a change from the past
    (B) The way in which it limits present-day science
    (C) The degree to which it has affected humans' reverence toward nature
    (D) The decisiveness with which it settled scientific disputes
    (E) The kinds of scientific discoveries on which it built

Choice **(A)** is correct. Both passages emphasize the extent to which Linnaeus' work represented a change from the past. Passage 1 discusses how "previous naturalists…had tried to name species by enumerating all of a species' distinguishing features" (lines 12–14). Linnaeus' innovations not only simplified the naming of species, but also "enabled scientists to retrieve information, make predictions, and understand traits by association" (lines 36–38). In Passage 2, the author expresses wariness "about the change [Linnaeus' system] has effected in humans' relationship to the world" (lines 79–80), explaining how from "Linnaeus on, much of science has been devoted to providing specific labels." The author believes that "the cost of having so successfully itemized and pigeonholed nature…is to limit certain possibilities of seeing and apprehending" (lines 84–88).

Choice (C) is incorrect. Passage 1 does not indicate one way or the other how Linnaeus' work *affected humans' reverence for nature*. Passage 2 discusses this subject, but only indirectly. The final paragraph points out that "modern humans have come to adopt the scientific view of the external world as a way of understanding their everyday experience in it." But, according to the author, this experience "is better understood as a synthesis…that is hopelessly beyond science's powers to analyze. It is quintessentially 'wild'…." The implication is that "modern humans" don't recognize the "external world" for what it is. They don't revere its "wild nature."

SAT I: Reasoning Test

Sunday, May 2000

1. Lacking self-assurance, he was too ------- to ------- controversial topics with people he did not know well.

   (A) impassioned . . analyze
   (B) timid . . discuss
   (C) cautious . . suppress
   (D) knowledgeable . . disregard
   (E) perceptive . . defend

Choice **(B)** is correct. The incomplete sentence indicates that this person lacked self-assurance or self-confidence. Someone lacking in self-confidence would probably be *timid* and unable to *discuss* topics that are likely to cause arguments with unfamiliar people.

Choice (C) is incorrect. The person described might be *cautious* due to his lack of self-confidence. However, a person who is *cautious* would probably try to *suppress* or hold back controversial topics, not avoid *suppressing* them.

2. After winning the lottery, John bought sports cars, built a mansion, and wore designer suits, but, by thus ------- his -------, he alienated his friends.

   (A) enduring . . hardship
   (B) flaunting . . prosperity
   (C) undermining . . image
   (D) calculating . . successes
   (E) moderating . . consumption

Choice **(B)** is correct. *Flaunting* something means showing it off, displaying it in ways that may suggest a feeling of superiority to other people. By *flaunting* his *prosperity*, John was displaying it in ways that offended his friends. To "alienate" your friends means to make them change their feelings toward you so that they are no longer your friends.

Choice (C) is incorrect. The words fail to fit both John's actions and the reactions of John's friends. *Undermining* or weakening his *image* does not describe John's purchases and display of his new wealth nor does the sentence suggest that John's friends felt any concern about his *image*.

3. Ballads often praise popular figures who have performed feats that many perceive as -------, such as defending the poor or resisting ------- authority.

   (A) modest . . acceptable
   (B) inescapable . . legitimate
   (C) insufficient . . overpowering
   (D) admirable . . unjust
   (E) unbelievable . . tolerable

Choice **(D)** is correct. The incomplete sentence suggests that popular characters in traditional songs often behave in ways that seem worthy of acclaim. The missing words should be consistent with that idea. Actions such as resisting *unjust* authority would be perceived by many people as *admirable*.

Choice (C) is incorrect. Popular characters in songs who opposed an *overpowering* authority might be seen as acting in a heroic and positive way, but an audience would be unlikely to consider their actions *insufficient*.

4. As ------- as the disintegration of the Roman Empire must have seemed, that disaster nevertheless presented some ------- aspects.

   (A) momentous . . formidable
   (B) decisive . . unavoidable
   (C) unexpected . . ambiguous
   (D) advantageous . . beneficial
   (E) catastrophic . . constructive

Choice **(E)** is correct. Word clues like "As…as" and "nevertheless" in the incomplete sentence signal that the correct choice must have words that contrast with each other. The disintegration of an empire seemed like a disaster and yet certain aspects were not disastrous. *Catastrophic* describes the way disastrous events must have appeared at the time. *Constructive* indicates that some aspects of the apparently disastrous event led to improvements or new developments.

Choice (C) is incorrect. *Ambiguous* means open to more than one interpretation. In this sentence, describing aspects as *ambiguous* indicates that the aspects were not clearly good or bad, which does not present a contrast to an apparent disaster. *Unexpected* also fails to fit the logic of the sentence since "that disaster" requires a word that indicates some great misfortune.

5. Predictably, detail-oriented workers are ------- keeping track of the myriad particulars of a situation.

   (A) remiss in
   (B) adept at
   (C) humorous about
   (D) hesitant about
   (E) contemptuous of

Choice **(B)** is correct. *Adept* means highly skilled. The words "myriad particulars" refer to a very large quantity of details. Workers who are "detailed-oriented" pay careful attention to details and would indeed be highly skilled at tracking a very large quantity of details in a situation.

Choice (E) is incorrect. "Predictably" signals that the missing word should be consistent with "detailed-oriented workers." Such workers would pay careful attention to the very large quantity of details in a situation, not be *contemptuous* or disdainful of them.

6. The beauty of Mount McKinley is usually cloaked: clouds ------- the summit nine days out of ten.

   (A) release
   (B) elevate
   (C) entangle
   (D) shroud
   (E) attain

Choice **(D)** is correct. The first part of the sentence indicates that the second part must describe the way that clouds hide a mountaintop. To *shroud* something is to hide it from view.

Choice (C) is incorrect. Although cloud formations might appear to *entangle* a mountaintop, *entangle* does not indicate that the clouds hide the mountaintop from view.

7. In the opening scene, the playwright creates such a strong impression of the ------- of the main characters that none of their subsequent, apparently honorable actions can ------- these characters in the eyes of the audience.

    (A) integrity . . discredit
    (B) conviction . . justify
    (C) corruption . . redeem
    (D) dignity . . excuse
    (E) degradation . . convict

Choice **(C)** is correct. The incomplete sentence suggests that the main characters of the play behave very badly at the beginning; none of the honorable actions those characters do later in the play can change the audience's first impressions. *Corruption* identifies the negative nature of the early behavior of the main characters. The statement that good deeds cannot *redeem* the main characters is consistent with the audience's unchanging disapproval.

Choice (A) is incorrect. *Integrity* means honesty, but the sentence indicates that, at the beginning of the play, the characters behave in ways that are far from honorable. To *discredit* characters is to disgrace them, to make them seem worse than they previously seemed. *Discredit* is illogical because this part of the sentence requires a word that means improving the reputation of the characters.

8. By allowing one printer to be used by several computers, this device ------- the need for many separate printers.

    (A) accelerates
    (B) predetermines
    (C) substantiates
    (D) precludes
    (E) anticipates

Choice **(D)** is correct. To *preclude* something is to rule it out. The device described in the sentence rules out the need for each computer to have its own, separate printer.

Choice (C) is incorrect. To *substantiate* something is confirm it. The device does the opposite of confirming the need for separate printers for each computer.

9. In an attempt to malign and misrepresent their opponents, some candidates resort to -------.

    (A) arbitration
    (B) narcissism
    (C) calumny
    (D) tenacity
    (E) solicitude

Choice **(C)** is correct. *Calumny* involves making false statements in order to damage someone's reputation. By maligning and misrepresenting opponents, the candidates are spreading untrue stories in an attempt to damage the reputations of their opponents.

Choice (B) is incorrect. *Narcissism* involves being extremely self-centered, being interested in yourself more than in anything else. Choice (B) does not demonstrate a process of maligning and misrepresenting the opponents.

10. GAZE : OBSERVER ::

    (A) hear : listener
    (B) banish : exile
    (C) separate : joint
    (D) operate : doctor
    (E) sprain : ankle

Choice **(A)** is correct. An OBSERVER by definition GAZEs at something, just as a *listener* by definition *hears* something.

Choice (D) is incorrect. To *operate*, in this context, is to perform surgery on a person. While some *doctors* perform surgery, this is not necessarily true of all *doctors*. So you could not say that a *doctor* by definition *operates*.

11. ODOMETER : DISTANCE ::

    (A) microscope : size
    (B) decibel : loudness
    (C) orchestra : instrument
    (D) computer : data
    (E) scale : weight

Choice **(E)** is correct. An ODOMETER is an instrument in a vehicle that indicates how far the vehicle has traveled. An ODOMETER is an instrument that measures DISTANCE, just as a *scale* is an instrument that measures *weight*.

Choice (B) is incorrect. A *decibel* is a unit of measure that indicates the *loudness* of a sound. Although the *loudness* of something can be measured in *decibels*, a *decibel* is not an instrument that measures *loudness*.

12. COPYRIGHT : BOOK ::

    (A) franchise : license
    (B) lease : owner
    (C) patent : design
    (D) trademark : registration
    (E) brand : manufacturer

Choice **(C)** is correct. A COPYRIGHT grants the legal right to publish and distribute a literary, dramatic, or musical work. A *patent* grants the legal right to make or sell an invention. The owner of the COPYRIGHT on a BOOK holds the rights to its distribution, just as the owner of a *patent* on a *design* holds the rights to its distribution.

Choice (E) is incorrect. A *brand* is a trademark or name identifying a class of goods made by a single company. A *manufacturer* owns a *brand*. You would not say, though, that a BOOK owns a COPYRIGHT.

13. FEIGN : DECEIVE ::

    (A) flee : elude
    (B) dangle : drop
    (C) send : receive
    (D) contract : lengthen
    (E) publish : write

Choice **(A)** is correct. To FEIGN is to pretend, or to give a false appearance of something. To FEIGN is to attempt to DECEIVE someone, just as to *flee* is to attempt to *elude* someone.

Choice (E) is incorrect. People might try to *publish* something that they *write*, but you would not say that to *publish* is to attempt to *write* someone.

14. ETHOS : VALUES ::

- (A) accord : nations
- **(B) code : principles**
- (C) policy : officials
- (D) debate : opinions
- (E) offense : criminals

Choice **(B)** is correct. The word ETHOS refers to the basic character or the fundamental beliefs of a person, a group of people, a culture, or an institution. A *code*, in this context, is a systematic set of *principles* governing conduct. An ETHOS is a set of fundamental VALUES, just as a *code* is a set of fundamental *principles*.

Choice (D) is incorrect. A *debate* involves an exchange of *opinions*. People present and defend their *opinions* during a *debate*—a *debate* is not a set of fundamental *opinions*.

15. TORPID : SLUGGISH ::

- (A) wrong : apologetic
- (B) refracted : direct
- **(C) comic : funny**
- (D) sad : empathetic
- (E) merry : morose

Choice **(C)** is correct. TORPID means lacking in energy. SLUGGISH means characterized by slow movements. Something that is TORPID is SLUGGISH, just as something that is *comic* is *funny*.

Choice (E) is incorrect. *Morose* means gloomy, which is the opposite of *merry*. Someone who is *merry* is by definition not *morose*.

16. In lines 1–5, Waverly characterizes June's advertisement as being

- **(A) unsophisticated and heavy-handed**
- (B) somber and convoluted
- (C) clear and concise
- (D) humorous and effective
- (E) clever and lively

Choice **(A)** is correct. In lines 1–5, Waverly, "in a deep television-announcer voice" reads the advertisement that June wrote. The italicization of the word "*three*" helps to emphasize the repetitive, plodding phrasing of June's advertisement. Furthermore, Waverly's exaggerated pronunciation of the word "*guaranteed*," again signaled by the use of italics, suggests that the advertisement is heavy-handed in its approach, and lacking in refinement and subtlety. This assessment is reinforced by June's mother's comment to Waverly in reference to her daughter: "True, one can't teach style. June is not sophisticated like you" (lines 9–10).

Choice (D) is incorrect. Although lines 1–5 contain references to laughter or describe events that evoke laughter, the lines do not indicate that Waverly views June's advertisement as *humorous and effective*. This characterization most aptly applies to Waverly's actions and the effect they evoke. It is Waverly's performance that is *humorous and effective*.

17. In the context of the passage, the statement "I was surprised at myself" (line 12) suggests that June

    (A) had been unaware of the extent of her emotional vulnerability
    (B) was exasperated that she allowed Waverly to embarrass her in public
    (C) was amazed that she could dislike anyone so much
    (D) had not realized that her mother admired her friend Waverly
    (E) felt guilty about how much she resented her own mother

Choice **(A)** is correct. In the statement, "I was surprised at myself," June acknowledges that she is caught off guard by her reaction to the events described in the previous two paragraphs. June indicates that she feels "humiliated" (line 12) and is bothered by being "outsmarted by Waverly once again" (line 13). She even feels "betrayed by [her] own mother" (line 14). Collectively, in the context of the passage, these comments and reactions reveal June's emotional vulnerability.

Choice **(B)** is incorrect. This choice is appealing because it is partially true. As she admits in line 12, June did feel "embarrassed." It is reasonable to assume that she might have feelings of exasperation or anger towards Waverly. However, in the context of the passage, this choice does not capture June's feelings of being "surprised." June's comments and reactions are not evidence of exasperation.

18. For June, a significant aspect of what happened at the dinner party is that

    (A) her mother had taken great pains to make Waverly feel welcome
    (B) her mother had criticized her for arguing with Waverly
    (C) her mother had sided against her in front of family and friends
    (D) Waverly had angered June's mother
    (E) Waverly had lied to June's mother

Choice **(C)** is correct. June states in line 14 that she feels "betrayed" by her mother's actions. The actual betrayal, as June characterizes it, occurs in lines 9–11, when her mother says to Waverly, "True, one can't teach style. June is not sophisticated like you. She must have been born this way." In front of family and friends, June's mother has supported Waverly, not June; therefore, June feels "betrayed."

Choice **(A)** is incorrect. Although June's mother's actions might be construed as a means of welcoming Waverly, this choice does not demonstrate how the incident affected June.

19. The description of June's encounter with the bartender primarily serves to suggest that

    (A) the relationship of mother and son is different from that of mother and daughter
    (B) June is not the only one who ponders the meaning of a jade pendant
    (C) a jade pendant symbolizes the mystery of life and death
    (D) June finally understands the true meaning of her jade pendant
    (E) strangers are easier to talk to than family members and friends

Choice **(B)** is correct. This choice is directly supported by information in lines 50–62, in which June describes her encounter with the bartender. His response to June's questions in lines 52 and 54 indicates that he is not certain why his mother gave him his pendant. "She gave it to me after I got divorced. I guess my mother's telling me I'm still worth something." The bartender's use of the word "guess" conveys feelings of uncertainty. Furthermore, June explicitly states that she knew "by the wonder in his voice that he had no idea what the pendant really meant" (lines 61–62).

Choice **(D)** is incorrect. Nothing in the passage indicates that June learns the true meaning of her pendant. In fact, lines 25–28 suggest the opposite. Only her mother, who is deceased, could have told June about her "life's importance." June wonders about the significance of the bartender's pendant, but she does not know the true meaning of her own pendant.

20. The passage indicates that the act of giving a jade pendant can best be described as

   (A) a widely observed tradition
   (B) a mother's plea for forgiveness
   (C) an example of a mother's extravagance
   (D) an unprecedented act of generosity
   (E) an unremarkable event in June's life

Choice **(A)** is correct. In lines 43–45, June mentions that she always notices "other people wearing these same jade pendants." She then describes the wearers of these pendants as being "sworn to the same secret covenant" (lines 48–49). From these statements, it is obvious that the giving of jade pendants is a common practice or *a widely observed tradition*.

Choice (D) is incorrect. While the giving of the pendant is an expression of *generosity*, it is not, according to the passage, an *unprecedented* act. Something that is *unprecedented* is novel, having no former example. June indicates seeing several people wearing these pendants.

21. The author's main point about the relationship between art and politics is that

   (A) Auden's view of the role of art is more widely accepted than the view that art is dangerous
   (B) Auden's denial of the political impact of art is somewhat misleading
   (C) artists such as Auden and Yeats incorporate political concerns in their art
   (D) artists and the people who admire their creations have different ideas about the political role of art
   (E) politicians suppress art that has the potential to cause undesirable political changes

Choice **(B)** is correct. The author's perspective on the "relationship between art and politics" becomes apparent in the last paragraph of the passage. In lines 66–68, the author writes "Indeed, construing art, as Auden does, as a causally or politically neutered activity is itself an act of neutralization." Later, in lines 68–73, the author indicates that "Representing art as something that in its nature can make nothing happen is not so much a view opposed to the view that art is dangerous as it is a way of responding to the sensed danger of art by treating art as though it were nothing to be afraid of." This comment implies that Auden's characterization of the relationship between art and politics is inaccurate, dubiously motivated, and thus misleading.

Choice (D) is incorrect. It is not clear from the passage that artists and those who admire their work necessarily differ in opinion about the political role of art. And, the main focus of the passage is not on the existence of such a difference.

22. Auden believed that artists and politicians would "get along better at a time of crisis" (lines 11–12) if politicians would

   (A) heed the messages that artists convey through art
   (B) remember the contributions that artists have made to culture through the ages
   (C) admit that art speaks in a language that is incomprehensible to politicians
   (D) recognize that art does not affect the course of history
   (E) acknowledge the role of artists in shaping the consciousness of a nation

Choice **(D)** is correct. This choice, directly supported by the quote attributed to Auden in lines 11–16, most closely paraphrases Auden's belief that "artists and politicians would get along better…if the latter would only realize that the political history of the world would have been the same if not a poem had been written, nor a picture painted, nor a bar of music composed."

Choice (E) is incorrect. This choice directly contradicts Auden's claim in lines 11–16. According to Auden, art does not influence history. It is quite unlikely, then, that Auden believed that artists could shape the consciousness of a nation.

23. The author emphasizes the word "already" (line 38) in order to stress the point that

   (A) Picasso's painting was perceived as just another artist's depiction of war
   (B) Picasso's political attitudes were widely known
   (C) Picasso's painting did not cause a change in political attitudes
   (D) Picasso did not expect his painting to be so controversial
   (E) Picasso had not thought his painting would be so quickly acclaimed

Choice **(C)** is correct. In lines 24–39, the author places the painting *Guernica* in a historical context. This section also includes commentary about the viewers who originally "paid money for the privilege of filing past" (line 37) the painting. According to the author, these individuals used the painting "as a mirror to reflect attitudes *already* in place" (line 38). In emphasizing the word "already," the author asserts that the viewers were not viewing the painting with new eyes, but with preconceived notions and established attitudes.

Choice (A) is incorrect. The author does not discuss other paintings that depict images of war, nor does the author suggest that *Guernica* was perceived as one of many works with a similar theme.

24. The author refers to "art-historical knowledge" (lines 39–40) in order to emphasize which point about Picasso's *Guernica*?

   (A) Most art historians share Auden's view of art.
   (B) The original purpose of the painting gradually became obscure.
   (C) The painting continues to memorialize those who were killed in the bombing of Guernica.
   (D) Art historians continue to discuss the artistic merits of the painting.
   (E) The Museum of Modern Art is an appropriate setting for the painting.

Choice **(B)** is correct. This choice is directly supported by lines 39–40 of the passage where the author states that "in later years it required art-historical knowledge to know what was going on." General awareness of the original meaning and purpose of *Guernica*, namely to speak about the Nazi atrocity in Spain and to serve as a fundraising event for the Spanish victims, has faded. People with knowledge of art history know the painting's significance; to others, *Guernica* is merely an attractive arrangement of "gray and black harmonies."

Choice (C) is incorrect. Although the author states in lines 47–53 that the painting ultimately does nothing more than memorialize the event, the reference to "art-historical knowledge" helps make the point that, for the ordinary viewer, *Guernica* is simply a painting.

25. The tone of the description in lines 42–46 ("and it was . . . guests") is one of

   (A) sorrow
   (B) admiration
   (C) indifference
   (D) sympathy
   (E) sarcasm

Choice **(E)** is correct. In lines 42–46 of the passage, the author describes the painting as being attractive with its "gray and black harmonies." In fact, a copy of the painting is featured in an interior design magazine and serves as a decorative wall piece in a "sophisticated modern kitchen where fancy meals [are] concocted for bright and brittle guests" (lines 45–46). The characterization of the meals as "fancy" and the guests as "bright and brittle" suggests that the author finds the situation ridiculous.

Choice (B) is incorrect. This answer might initially seem correct because the author does indicate in lines 42–43 that the painting is "sufficiently attractive in its gray and black harmonies." However, the question is ultimately about the tone in lines 42–46 and requires recognition of how the author views the guests, as well as the use to which the painting is put.

26. In discussing Picasso's *Guernica*, the author indicates that the painting's ultimate accomplishment was

    (A)   providing a politically effective condemnation of an atrocity
    (B)   heightening political consciousness among its viewers
    (C)   commemorating a terrible event
    (D)   gaining Picasso recognition as a political activist
    (E)   revealing the versatility of Picasso's artistic talent

Choice **(C)** is correct. In lines 47–53, the author indicates that the painting did not change political thinking or help the people for which it was intended. It simply memorialized, enshrined, and spiritualized an event.

Choice (A) is incorrect. The author's discussion of *Guernica* directly contradicts the notion that the painting was effective as a political condemnation of the Nazi atrocity.

27. The author would probably characterize "some" (line 54) as being

    (A)   understandably content to follow a practical course of action
    (B)   relieved that a difficult decision has been made
    (C)   agreeable to a compromise that would weaken the author's argument
    (D)   reluctant to compare the concerns of artists with those of politicians
    (E)   convinced that art has a limited political role

Choice **(E)** is correct. This choice is best supported by the passage and best captures the relationship between lines 47–53 and line 54. In lines 47–53, the author states that *Guernica* ultimately fell short of its intention; it only commemorated an event. "Some," in the statement "Fine, some would say" (line 54), are individuals who agree with the notion that *Guernica*, Auden's poetry, and art in general, can do little in the real, practical world, the world of politics and action.

Choice (C) is incorrect. This choice might seem appealing because the statement "Fine, some would say" suggests agreement. There is no indication, however, that what "some" would agree with is a compromise or a resolution of differences.

28. In line 68, the word "neutralization" refers to an act of

    (A)   making objective
    (B)   blending with something that counteracts
    (C)   bringing to destruction
    (D)   rendering ineffective
    (E)   prohibiting conflict

Choice **(D)** is correct. Lines 66–68 of the passage best support this response. According to the author, "construing art, as Auden does, as a causally or politically neutered activity is itself an act of neutralization." In other words, to argue that art lacks practical or political potency is, in effect, an attempt to render art ineffective.

Choice (B) is incorrect. Although the process of "neutralization" could entail the blending of one thing with another to counteract an effect—for example, giving an antidote to counter the effects of a poison—the question asks for the reference of "neutralization," not the direct meaning, in the context of the sentence in lines 66–68.

29. The author concludes that "Representing art as something that in its nature can make nothing happen" (lines 68–70) is actually

(A) proof that art is subversive
(B) an activity that in itself is inconsequential
(C) the only valid response to art
(D) a reaction to perceptions about art's power
(E) an act of defiance in response to political pressures

Choice **(D)** is correct. This response is best supported by lines 68–73: "Representing art as something that in its nature can make nothing happen is not so much a view opposed to the view that art is dangerous as it is a way of responding to the sensed danger of art by treating art as though it were nothing to be afraid of." From the author's perspective, Auden recognizes that art indeed does have a power and, being fearful of that power, tries to neutralize it by treating art as if it were harmless and ineffective.

Choice (A) is incorrect. This choice is attractive in light of the last paragraph (lines 54–73) where art is described in terms of being dangerous. By definition, that which is *subversive* has the ability to destroy and is thus dangerous, but the author does not conclude that representing art as ineffective is *proof* that art is subversive. Instead, the author concludes that such a representation is actually an acknowledgement of the danger art can pose to the established political order.

30. The author's strategy in the passage is best described as

(A) relating an incident and then explaining its significance
(B) refuting an argument and then examining a counterargument
(C) presenting a position and then criticizing it
(D) summarizing an achievement and then analyzing it
(E) describing several examples and then explaining how they differ from one another

Choice **(C)** is correct. In lines 1–53, the author presents information about Auden's position on the relationship between art and politics. Picasso's *Guernica* is used as an example to illustrate Auden's belief that art is powerless to bring about real change. In lines 54–58, the author asks, "But if the sole political role of poetry is this deflected, consolatory, ceremonial ... office, why is the political attitude that art is dangerous so pervasive in our society?" The author then suggests that art really does have a power (lines 68–73) and the characterization of art as ineffective is an attempt to neutralize it. These comments implicitly criticize Auden's position.

Choice (B) is incorrect. There is no refutation of the argument that art is powerless. No specific examples of art's power are indicated, only a suggestion that those who say art is powerless may do so because they fear the opposite is true. Furthermore, there is no examination of the view that art is powerful, only a statement of it.

1. If $n+n+n+n+1=2+n+n+n$, what is the value of n ?

   (A) 1
   (B) 2
   (C) 3
   (D) 4
   (E) 7

Choice **(A)** is correct. To solve this equation, subtract three ns from both sides of the equation: $n+1=2$ or $n=1$.

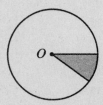

2. O is the center of the circle above. Approximately what percent of the circle is shaded?

   (A)   1%
   (B) 10%
   (C) 25%
   (D) 50%
   (E) 75%

Choice **(B)** is correct. Not enough information is given to determine the exact percentage that is shaded, so examine the options to help you estimate. The central angle of the shaded sector indicates what portion of the circle is shaded. Since one complete revolution is 360°, 1% of that would be only 3.6°, a very small angle. 10% is 36°, which is close to the angle shown. 25% is 90°, which appears too large.

3. Which of the following numbers is greater than 0.428 ?

   (A) 0.053
   (B) 0.42
   (C) 0.43
   (D) 0.419
   (E) 0.4228

Choice **(C)** is correct.
0.053 is less than 0.428 because in the tenths place $0 < 4$.
0.42 is less than 0.428 because there is an implied 0 in the thousandths place of 0.42 and $0 < 8$.
0.43 is greater than 0.428 because in the hundredths place $3 > 2$.
0.419 is less than 0.428 because in the hundredths place $1 < 2$.
0.4228 is less than 0.428 because in the thousandths place $2 < 8$.

Alternatively, for real numbers x and y, "x is greater than y" means that $x - y$ is positive. Of the five options given, only $0.43 - 0.428$ gives a positive difference.

4. Karen's salary is greater than Margot's but less than Henrietta's. If k, m, and h represent each of their salaries, respectively, which of the following is true?

(A) $h < k < m$
(B) $k < h < m$
(C) $k < m < h$
(D) $m < h < k$
(E) $m < k < h$

Choice **(E)** is correct. Karen's salary is greater than Margot's, or $m < k$. Karen's salary is less than Henrietta's, or $k < h$. Combining these two inequalities gives $m < k < h$.

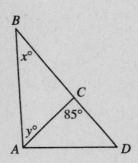

Note: Figure not drawn to scale.

5. In $\triangle ABD$ above, if $y = 40$, what is the value of x?

(A) 25
(B) 30
(C) 35
(D) 40
(E) 45

Choice **(E)** is correct. Line AC intersects line BD, creating adjacent angles $\angle ACB$ and $\angle ACD$, which are supplementary. The sum of their measures, then, is 180°. The measure of $\angle ACD$ is 85°.

$$85° + m\angle BCA = 180°$$
$$m\angle BCA = 95°$$

Since the sum of the measures of the three angles in a triangle is 180°, you can now find the value of x in triangle ABC.

$$x + y + 95 = 180$$
$$x + 40 + 95 = 180$$
$$x + 135 = 180$$
$$x = 45$$

6. Chuck is writing the page number on the bottom of each page of a 25-page book report, starting with 1. How many <u>digits</u> will he have written after he has written the number 25 ?

    (A) 35
    (B) 40
    (C) 41
    (D) 49
    (E) 50

Choice **(C)** is correct. Among the 25 integers from 1 to 25, the first 9 are one-digit integers and the remaining 16 are two-digit integers. So the total number of digits is 9×1 plus 16×2, which equals $9 + 32$ or 41.

7. Tim had $2b$ books for sale at a price of k dollars each. If y is the number of books he did <u>not</u> sell, which of the following represents the total dollar amount he received in sales from the books?

    (A) $k(2b - y)$

    (B) $k(y - 2b)$

    (C) $ky - 2b$

    (D) $2b - ky$

    (E) $2bk - y$

Choice **(A)** is correct. If Tim had $2b$ books for sale and did <u>not</u> sell y of them, then the number of books he sold was $2b - y$. Since he received k dollars for each of the books he sold, the total dollar amount he received in sales from the books was $k(2b - y)$.

Choice (E) is incorrect. The $2bk$ represents the dollar amount Tim would have received if he had sold all of the books. Then the <u>number</u> of books he did not sell, y, is subtracted from that amount. To obtain the amount he received in sales from the books, you must subtract the <u>price</u> of the unsold books from the dollar amount he would have received if he had sold all of the books.

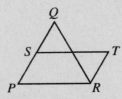

8. In the figure above, $\triangle PQR$ is equilateral and $PSTR$ is a parallelogram. If S is the midpoint of PQ and the perimeter of $\triangle PQR$ is 6, what is the perimeter of $PSTR$?

    (A) 9
    (B) 8
    (C) 6
    (D) 4
    (E) 3

Choice **(C)** is correct. Since $\triangle PQR$ is equilateral and its perimeter is 6, the length of PR is 2. The length of PS is 1 because S is the midpoint of PQ. The length of ST is 2 and the length of RT is 1 because $PSTR$ is a parallelogram and opposite sides of a parallelogram have equal lengths. The perimeter of $PSTR$ is $1 + 2 + 1 + 2$ or 6.

9. Five balls, each of radius $2\frac{1}{2}$ inches, are placed side by side in a straight row with adjacent balls touching. What is the distance, in inches, between the center of the first ball and the center of the last ball?

(A) 15

(B) $17\frac{1}{2}$

(C) 20

(D) $22\frac{1}{2}$

(E) 25

Choice **(C)** is correct. Drawing a figure of the situation described helps in solving this problem.

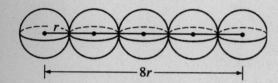

If the balls are lined up as described, you can see in the figure that there are 8 radii between the centers of the first and last balls in the row. $8 \times 2\frac{1}{2}$ inches $= 20$ inches.

10. The average (arithmetic mean) of nine numbers is 9. When a tenth number is added, the average of the ten numbers is also 9. What is the tenth number?

(A) 0

(B) $\frac{9}{10}$

(C) $\frac{10}{9}$

(D) 9

(E) 10

Choice **(D)** is correct. Since the average of the 9 numbers is 9, their sum is 81. If x is the tenth number, then $\frac{81+x}{10} = 9$. Solve this equation for x: $81 + x = 90$, or $x = 9$.

$$
\begin{array}{r}
1A \\
+ \ A \\
\hline
2B
\end{array}
$$

11. In the correctly solved addition problem above, A and B represent digits. If A is not equal to B, how many different digits from 0 through 9 could A represent?

(A) Two
(B) Three
(C) Five
(D) Seven
(E) Nine

Choice **(C)** is correct. Notice that since the answer is $2B$ rather than $1B$, a 1 must have been carried from the column with the A's to the next column. That means that $A \geq 5$, since any value less than 5 would not require that a 1 be carried.

For example, the addition problem could be $\begin{array}{r} 17 \\ + \ 7 \\ \hline 24 \end{array}$, but it could not be $\begin{array}{r} 13 \\ + \ 3 \\ \hline 16 \end{array}$.

Below is a table of all possible values for A and B.

A	B
5	0
6	2
7	4
8	6
9	8

Since A is never equal to B in the table, A has five possible values.

12. When 247 is divided by 6, the remainder is r, and when 247 is divided by 12, the remainder is s. What is the value of $r - s$?

(A) −6
(B) −1
(C) 0
(D) 1
(E) 6

Choice **(A)** is correct. First, divide 247 by 6 to find the remainder r.

$$
\begin{array}{r}
41 \\
6\overline{)247} \\
\underline{24} \ \ \\
07 \\
\underline{6} \\
1
\end{array}
$$

The remainder is 1, so $r = 1$. Then divide 247 by 12 to find the remainder s.

$$
\begin{array}{r}
20 \\
12\overline{)247} \\
\underline{24} \ \ \\
07 \\
\underline{0} \\
7
\end{array}
$$

The remainder is 7, so $s = 7$. The value of $r - s$ is $1 - (7) = -6$.

Questions 13-14 refer to the following coordinate system.

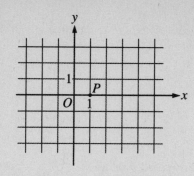

13. Point T (not shown) is located by beginning at P, moving 1 unit up and then moving 2 units to the right. What is the slope of line PT?

(A) $\dfrac{1}{3}$

(B) $\dfrac{1}{2}$

(C) 1

(D) 2

(E) 3

Choice **(B)** is correct. The slope of line PT can be found by choosing any two points on the line and calculating $\dfrac{\text{the change in } y}{\text{the change in } x}$ for these points. Since point T is obtained from point P by moving 1 unit up and 2 units to the right, $\dfrac{\text{the change in } y}{\text{the change in } x} = \dfrac{1}{2}$. Notice that it was not necessary to compute the coordinates of point T to find the slope here, but you could have approached the question in that manner. Point T has coordinates $(3,1)$.

14. Line ℓ (not shown) contains point P and has slope 5. Which of the following points is on line ℓ ?

(A) $(0, 5)$
(B) $(1, 5)$
(C) $(2, 5)$
(D) $(5, 1)$
(E) $(5, 5)$

Choice **(C)** is correct. Any two points on line ℓ must have coordinates such that $\dfrac{\text{the change in } y}{\text{the change in } x} = \dfrac{5}{1}$ since the slope of

line ℓ is 5. That is, if (a, b) and (c, d) are any two points on line ℓ, $\dfrac{d-b}{c-a} = 5$. Point P has coordinates $(1, 0)$, so let (a, b)

be $(1, 0)$. Try each of the choices as the second point (c, d). If choice (A) $(0, 5)$ is the second point, then

$\dfrac{d-b}{c-a} = \dfrac{5-0}{0-1} = \dfrac{5}{-1} = -5$, not 5. Likewise, if (c, d) were choice (B) $(1, 5)$, $\dfrac{d-b}{c-a} = \dfrac{5-0}{1-1} = \dfrac{5}{0}$, which is undefined. Notice

that $(1, 5)$ is directly above point P on the graph, so the line between $(1, 5)$ and P would be a vertical line, not a line with a slope of 5.

Choice (C) $(2, 5)$ yields $\dfrac{d-b}{c-a} = \dfrac{5-0}{2-1} = \dfrac{5}{1} = 5$, the desired slope. You can check choices (D) and (E) to see that they do not

yield a slope of 5.

Another approach to this question would be to find the equation of line ℓ. The point-slope form of the equation of this line is given by $y - 0 = 5(x - 1)$, which simplifies to $y = 5x - 5$. Of the choices given, the only point whose coordinates satisfy this equation is the point $(2, 5)$.

15. The quantity $\left(3 \times 8^{12}\right)$ is how many times the quantity $\left(3 \times 8^{5}\right)$?

(A) 7

(B) 8

(C) 21

(D) 8^{7}

(E) 3×8^{7}

Choice **(D)** is correct. This question is asking for the result of $\left(3 \times 8^{12}\right)$ divided by $\left(3 \times 8^{5}\right)$. In the division, the common factor 3 will cancel out. Using the rules for exponents, the exponents should be subtracted when $\left(8^{12}\right)$ is divided by $\left(8^{5}\right)$, which equals 8^{7}. If you failed to cancel the 3s, you would arrive at choice (E), but when $\left(3 \times 8^{5}\right)$ is multiplied by $\left(3 \times 8^{7}\right)$, the product is $\left(9 \times 8^{12}\right)$, not $\left(3 \times 8^{12}\right)$.

16. The dogs in a certain kennel are fed Brand A and Brand B dog food only. Of these dogs, 6 dogs eat Brand A and 15 dogs eat Brand B. If 4 of the dogs that eat Brand B also eat Brand A, how many dogs are in the kennel?

(A) 17
(B) 19
(C) 21
(D) 25
(E) 29

Choice **(A)** is correct. Since every dog in the kennel eats Brand A, Brand B, or both brands of dog food, the total number of dogs can be found by adding the number that eat each brand and then subtracting the number that eat both brands, so that those who eat both will not be counted twice. The number of dogs who eat Brand A is 6; the number who eat Brand B is 15, and 4 dogs eat both brands. The number of dogs in the kennel is then $6 + 15 - 4 = 17$.

Choice (C) is incorrect. The number of dogs in the kennel is <u>not</u> equal to the sum of the number of dogs that eat each brand of dog food, which is $6 + 15 = 21$. The 4 dogs that eat both brands are counted twice in this sum.

17. On a number line, point A has coordinate -3 and point B has coordinate 12. Point P is $\dfrac{2}{3}$ of the way from A to B. What is the coordinate of point P?

(A) -1
(B) 2
(C) 6
(D) 7
(E) 10

Choice **(D)** is correct. It may be helpful to sketch a number line and mark 0 and the points A and B. This will help you see that the length of AB is 15.

$$
\begin{array}{ccccc}
 & A & & P & B \\
\hline
-5 & & 0 & 5 & 10
\end{array}
$$

Since $\dfrac{2}{3}(15) = 10$, point P is 10 units to the right of point A, so it has a coordinate of $-3 + 10 = 7$.

18. If the ratio of two positive integers is 3 to 2, which of the following statements about these integers CANNOT be true?

  (A) Their sum is an odd integer.
  (B) Their sum is an even integer.
  (C) Their product is divisible by 6.
  (D) Their product is an even integer.
  (E) Their product is an odd integer.

Choice **(E)** is correct. If the ratio of two positive integers is 3 to 2, let $3x$ and $2x$ represent these integers, where x is some positive integer. The sum of the two integers is $3x + 2x = 5x$. The product of the two integers is $(3x)(2x) = 6x^2$.

(A) Can $5x$ be odd? Yes, if x is odd.

(B) Can $5x$ be even? Yes, if x is even.

(C) Can $6x^2$ be divisible by 6? Yes, it is divisible by 6 for any value of x.

(D) Can $6x^2$ be even? Yes, it must be even because it is divisible by 6 and 6 is divisible by 2.

(E) Can $6x^2$ be odd? No.

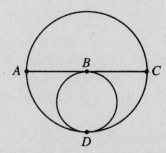

19. In the figure above, B is the center of the larger circle. The smaller circle is tangent to the larger circle at D and contains point B. If the length of diameter AC is 12, what is the area of the smaller circle?

  (A) 6π
  (B) 9π
  (C) 12π
  (D) 16π
  (E) 36π

Choice **(B)** is correct. If the diameter of the larger circle is 12, then its radius is 6. Segment BD is both a radius of the larger circle and a diameter of the smaller circle, so the radius of the smaller circle is 3. It follows that the area of the smaller circle is $A = \pi r^2 = \pi(3)^2 = 9\pi$.

x	1	2	3	4
y	$\dfrac{(0)(2)}{3}$	$\dfrac{(1)(3)}{5}$	$\dfrac{(2)(4)}{7}$	$\dfrac{(3)(5)}{9}$

20. Of the following equations, which describes the relationship between x and y in the table above?

(A) $y = \dfrac{2x-2}{x+2}$

(B) $y = \dfrac{2x-1}{x+3}$

(C) $y = \dfrac{(x-1)(x+1)}{2x+1}$

(D) $y = \dfrac{(x-1)(2x-2)}{2x+1}$

(E) $y = \dfrac{2^x}{2x+1}$

Choice **(C)** is correct. In the table, the values of y are given in a form that suggests the pattern relating x to y — the numerators of the fractions are given in factored form. What kind of pattern exists between the x value and the two factors? Notice that in each case the first factor is 1 less than the value of x and the second factor is 1 more than the value of x. This suggests that the numerator of the fraction is equal to $(x-1)(x+1)$. The relationship between the value of x and the denominator is that the denominator is 1 more than twice the value of x; that is, it equals $2x+1$. Hence $y = \dfrac{(x-1)(x+1)}{2x+1}$.

Choice (A) is incorrect. This choice gives the correct value for y when x is 1, but not when x is 2. Other choices may be correct for one or more of the values in the table, but not for all of them.

21. S is the sum of the first 100 consecutive positive <u>even</u> integers, and T is the sum of the first 100 consecutive positive integers. S is what percent greater than T?

(A) **100%**
(B) 50%
(C) 10%
(D) 2%
(E) 1%

Choice **(A)** is correct. $S = 2+4+6+\cdots+200$ and $T = 1+2+3+\cdots+100$. In particular $S = 2T$, since every term in the sum S is twice the corresponding term in the sum T. So $S = T + T$, which means that S is T greater than T. S is 100 percent greater than T because T is equal to 100 percent of T. Be careful to note that the equation $S = 2T$ means that S is 200 percent <u>of</u> T, but it also means that S is 100 percent <u>greater than</u> T.

Product	Number of People Choosing Product
W	37
X	51
Y	m
Z	n

22. The table above shows the results of a survey of 200 people in which each person chose exactly 1 of 4 products. If m and n are positive integers, what is the greatest possible value of n ?

(A) 12
(B) 56
(C) 111
(D) 112
(E) 200

Choice **(C)** is correct. According to the survey, 200 people were polled. Therefore, the number of people choosing products W, X, Y, and Z should add up to 200. It is given that 37 people chose product W and 51 people chose product X. The sum of 51 and 37 gives the number of people accounted for so far in the survey: $51 + 37 = 88$. Subtracting that number from the total number of people surveyed gives the sum of m and n. That is, $m + n = 112$. Since m and n are both positive integers, the smallest possible number that m could be is 1. Substituting 1 for m gives n its greatest possible value of 111.

23. If $kn \neq k$ and $n = \dfrac{1}{k}$, which of the following expressions is equivalent to $\dfrac{1-k}{1-n}$?

(A) $-n$
(B) $-k$
(C) 1
(D) k
(E) n

Choice **(B)** is correct. Since n is equal to $\dfrac{1}{k}$, substitute $\dfrac{1}{k}$ in the expression $\dfrac{1-k}{1-n}$ to get $\dfrac{1-k}{1-\dfrac{1}{k}}$. To simplify this expression,

multiply by $\dfrac{k}{k}$, which simplifies the expression to $\dfrac{k(1-k)}{k-1}$. The quantity $(1-k)$ can be written $(-1)(k-1)$, so the

fraction is equivalent to $\dfrac{k(-1)(k-1)}{(k-1)}$. This fraction can be further simplified by dividing both the numerator and the

denominator by the common factor $(k-1)$, giving $k(-1)$, or $-k$, as the simplified form of the fraction.

The statement that $kn \neq k$, given at the beginning of the question, assures you that k is not zero and that n is not 1, so it is permissible to divide by k or $(n-1)$.

Choice (C) is incorrect. It is possible to arrive at this answer if you cancel incorrectly. In a fraction, you can cancel a factor that appears in both the numerator and the denominator. Although 1 appears in both the numerator and denominator in the original expression, it does not appear as a factor, so canceling the 1s is an invalid step.

24. The first two numbers of a sequence are 1 and 3, respectively. The third number is 4, and, in general, every number after the second is the sum of the two numbers immediately preceding it. How many of the first 1,000 numbers in this sequence are odd?

(A) 333
(B) 500
(C) 665
(D) 666
(E) 667

Choice **(E)** is correct. First, find several more numbers in the sequence. Using the rule described, the sequence would be 1, 3, 4, 7, 11, 18, 29, 47, etc. To find out how many of the numbers in the sequence are odd, it is not necessary to compute the values of all of the numbers. Instead, notice the pattern of even and odd numbers: the first two numbers in the sequence, 1 and 3, are both odd. The third number in the sequence is even because the sum of two odd numbers is always even. The fourth number in the sequence is the sum of an odd number and an even number, so it is odd. The fifth number is the sum of an even and an odd number, so it is odd also. The sixth number, like the third number, is again the sum of two odd numbers, so it is even. The pattern for the sequence, which continues indefinitely, is odd, odd, even, odd, odd, even, and so

forth in groups of three. Of the first 999 numbers in the sequence, two out of three or $\frac{2}{3}$ of them are odd and $\frac{1}{3}$ of them are

even. That is, $\frac{2}{3} \times 999 = 666$ of these numbers are odd. The 1,000[th] number is also odd, so there are a total of 667 odd

numbers in the first 1,000 numbers of the sequence.

25. Circle C has radius $\sqrt{2}$. Squares with sides of length 1 are to be drawn so that, for each square, one vertex is on circle C and the rest of the square is inside circle C. What is the greatest number of such squares that can be drawn if the squares do not have overlapping areas?

(A) None
(B) One
(C) Two
(D) Three
(E) Four

Choice **(E)** is correct. Squares with sides of length 1 have diagonals of length $\sqrt{2}$. Since one vertex of each square must be on circle C, and the rest of the square must be inside the circle, making the diagonals of the squares radii of the circle will help to fit as many squares as possible into the circle.

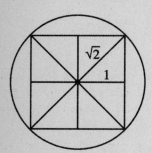

Since one vertex of the square is at the center of the circle and there are 360° around the center of the circle, it is possible to draw four 90° angles around the center of the circle, and thus, four squares.

1. The stage director insisted that before the next performance the set be ------- to eliminate its dinginess.

    (A) requisitioned
    (B) enlarged
    (C) refurbished
    (D) demolished
    (E) relocated

Choice **(C)** is correct. To *refurbish* something is to make it clean, bright, or fresh again. "Dinginess" is the quality of being dirty or discolored. *Refurbishing* a stage set would make it clean and bright again, thus "eliminating its dinginess."

Choice (B) is incorrect. To *enlarge* something is to increase its size by adding new material to the existing material. If a dirty or discolored set were *enlarged* by the addition of new material, its overall appearance might or might not be improved, but the condition of the original material would remain unchanged. The set's "dinginess" would not be eliminated.

2. Most pioneers ------- this valley on their journey to the West because its rugged terrain and frequent landslides made it a ------- place for travelers.

    (A) flanked . . fascinating
    (B) avoided . . necessary
    (C) encompassed . . curious
    (D) enjoyed . . troublesome
    (E) skirted . . hazardous

Choice **(E)** is correct. To *skirt* something is to go around it rather than across or through it. Something that is *hazardous* presents a danger. A valley with a "rugged terrain and frequent landslides" would present a danger to travelers, so pioneers would most likely wish to go around rather than through it.

Choice (A) is incorrect. To *flank* something is to place oneself at the side of it. Something that is *fascinating* is of great interest. Having a "rugged terrain and frequent landslides" would not necessarily make a valley a place of great interest to travelers. And, even if such a valley were of great interest to the pioneers, that would give them reason to venture into it rather than merely stand at the side of it.

3. Most people would be amazed to discover how ------- their recollections are, even those memories of which they are most -------.

    (A) unpleasant . . frightened
    (B) repressed . . unaware
    (C) inaccurate . . certain
    (D) amorphous . . unsure
    (E) trustworthy . . confident

Choice **(C)** is correct. In general, amazement is caused by encountering something very unexpected. People who are *certain* of particular memories fully expect these recollections to be accurate reflections of the past. If such people were to discover that their recollections were in fact *inaccurate*, they would encounter something unexpected and so might naturally be amazed.

Choice (B) is incorrect. A *repressed* recollection is a memory that has been pushed out of the conscious mind and into a part of the psyche that lies below the threshold of awareness. It is to be expected, then, that people are completely *unaware* of their *repressed* memories. Hence, while people might be amazed to learn that some of their recollections have been *repressed*, they would not be at all amazed to discover that these are the memories of which they are most *unaware*.

4. Perhaps the most visible sign of the ------- nature of the Cherokee nation was the fact that the women who led each clan picked the chief.

    (A) stoic
    (B) matriarchal
    (C) defensive
    (D) caustic
    (E) didactic

Choice **(B)** is correct. A *matriarchal* society is one in which a woman or group of women rules or has great influence. To lead a clan and pick its chief is to have a great influence on society. The fact that women fulfilled these functions in the Cherokee nation attests to its *matriarchal* nature.

Choice (A) is incorrect. To be *stoic* is to show indifference to pain or pleasure. The fact that Cherokee women led clans and selected chiefs reveals nothing about how the members of the Cherokee nation reacted to pain or pleasure and so gives no indication of whether they were *stoic* or not.

5. Castillo's poetry has generated only enthusiastic response: praise from the general public and ------- from the major critics.

    (A) condemnation
    (B) sarcasm
    (C) plaudits
    (D) irony
    (E) pathos

Choice **(C)** is correct. Because Castillo's poetry is said to have generated <u>only</u> enthusiastic response, both of the reactions mentioned after the colon must be examples of such a response. "Praise from the general public" clearly fits this description and so do "*plaudits* from the major critics." The word *plaudits* (closely related to the word *applaud* and almost always used in the plural) means enthusiastic approval.

Choice (E) is incorrect. *Pathos* is an emotion of sympathetic pity. If critics were to react to Castillo's poetry by feeling pity, their response would be sympathetic, not enthusiastic, as the logic of the sentence requires.

6. Many scientists have such specialized expertise that they look only at ------- aspects of nature, but ecologists are concerned with the ------- of the natural environment.

    (A) complex . . purity
    (B) detailed . . paradox
    (C) isolated . . totality
    (D) universal . . balance
    (E) distant . . erosion

Choice **(C)** is correct. The word "but" signals an opposition between the thoughts expressed in the first and second clauses of the sentence. The words inserted into the blanks must therefore support a contrast of ideas. The words *isolated* and *totality* do this. In the first clause, it makes sense to say that those with "specialized expertise" in science limit their interest to one particular field or *isolated* aspect of nature. A contrasting approach would be to take a broad interest in the entire natural environment, and this is what ecologists are said to do when *totality* is inserted into the blank in the second clause.

Choice (A) is incorrect. Looking only at *complex* aspects of nature is not incompatible with, or opposed to, a concern for the *purity* of the natural environment. This choice of words does not support the contrast of ideas that the logic of the sentence requires.

7. Notoriously ------- regarding issues of national security, the Prime Minister dumbfounded her opponents when she ------- a defense appropriations bill they had expected her to contest.

    (A) evenhanded . . muddled
    (B) compliant . . conceded on
    (C) pacific . . opposed
    (D) intransigent . . compromised on
    (E) rancorous . . railed against

Choice **(D)** is correct. To be *intransigent* is to refuse to *compromise*. When someone who is known to be *intransigent compromises*, that is cause for surprise or even astonishment. It makes sense, then, that the opponents of a notoriously *intransigent* Prime Minister would be "dumbfounded" (astonished) to learn that she had *compromised on* a bill.

Choice (B) is incorrect. To be *compliant* is to be disposed to make concessions during arguments or negotiations. If the Prime Minister were known to be *compliant*, it would not dumbfound her opponents to learn that she had *conceded on* a bill.

8. Leslie thoroughly -------- the text to avoid any lawsuits that might arise because of the new obscenity law.

    (A) condensed
    (B) delineated
    (C) exterminated
    (D) expurgated
    (E) transcribed

Choice **(D)** is correct. To *expurgate* a text is to remove offensive or obscene material from it prior to publication. If all obscene material were removed from a text, it would not very likely become the target of legal action based on an obscenity law. It makes sense, then, that Leslie would *expurgate* a text in order to avoid such lawsuits.

Choice (B) is incorrect. To *delineate* something is to describe it in general outline. Simply describing a text would not affect its content in any way and so would not prevent the text from becoming the target of an obscenity lawsuit. Thus, it would not make sense for Leslie to *delineate* a text as a means of avoiding lawsuits.

9. The skepticism of some ancient philosophers ------- and helps to elucidate varieties of nihilism that appeared in the early nineteenth century.

    (A) suppresses
    (B) disseminates
    (C) undermines
    (D) confounds
    (E) foreshadows

Choice **(E)** is correct. To *foreshadow* something is to provide an early indication of it, often in a way that elucidates or makes clear certain aspects of the later development. "Nihilism" is a doctrine or belief that all values are baseless and that nothing can be known or communicated. As an "ancient" philosophy, skepticism provides an early indication of the extreme form of skepticism known as nihilism that developed much later, "in the early nineteenth century."

Choice (B) is incorrect. While it is true that one philosophical system often influences another, it does not make sense to say that one *disseminates* the other. To *disseminate* something is to spread it abroad, as a newspaper, for instance, spreads the information it contains throughout a region. Since ancient skepticism does not contain the nihilism that appeared only much later, it cannot be said to spread that philosophy abroad.

10. The doctor ------- so frequently on disease-prevention techniques that her colleagues accused her of -------.

    (A) **vacillated . . inconsistency**
    (B) sermonized . . fidelity
    (C) wavered . . steadfastness
    (D) experimented . . inflexibility
    (E) relied . . negligence

Choice **(A)** is correct. To *vacillate* is to swing indecisively from one course of action or opinion to another. To change opinions frequently is a sure sign of *inconsistency*, the quality of being unpredictable and even self-contradictory. It makes sense that a doctor's frequent *vacillations* on questions of medical technique would lead to charges of *inconsistency*.

Choice (E) is incorrect. To *rely* on a technique is to use it with confidence. *Negligence*, in a medical context, is the failure to exercise proper care or caution in treating a patient. A doctor who confidently used disease-prevention techniques would indeed be exercising considerable care and caution in treating patients and so could not reasonably be accused of medical *negligence*.

11. RULER : LINE ::

    (A) stamp : letter
    (B) period : dot
    (C) key : door
    (D) **compass : circle**
    (E) thermometer : degree

Choice **(D)** is correct. A RULER is a strip of material with a straight edge for drawing lines. A *compass* is an adjustable V-shaped device with a point on one end and a pencil on the other that is used to trace the form of a *circle* or a circular arc. A RULER is a device used to draw a LINE, just as a *compass* is a device used to draw a *circle*.

Choice (E) is incorrect. A *thermometer* is an instrument used to measure temperature in *degree* units, but a *thermometer* is not a device used to draw a *degree*.

12. CATNAP : SLEEP ::

    (A) exhaustion : slumber
    (B) blink : eye
    (C) **snack : meal**
    (D) swallow : bite
    (E) feast : banquet

Choice **(C)** is correct. A CATNAP is a brief period of light SLEEP. A *snack* is a hurried or light *meal*. CATNAP refers to a brief or light SLEEP, just as *snack* refers to a brief or light *meal*.

Choice (A) is incorrect. The word *slumber* has a meaning similar to that of SLEEP, but you are not supposed to look for words with similar meanings—you are supposed to look for <u>pairs</u> of words with similar <u>relationships</u>. Being exhausted may cause one to *slumber*, but *exhaustion* does not refer to a brief or light *slumber*.

13. MANAGER : STORE ::

    (A)   technician : laboratory
    (B)   student : school
    (C)   administrator : hospital
    (D)   spectator : arena
    (E)   president : electorate

Choice **(C)** is correct. A MANAGER and an *administrator* are both people who direct or control something or are in charge of something. The person in charge of a STORE is a MANAGER, just as the person in charge of a *hospital* is an *administrator*.

Choice (A) is incorrect. A *technician* may work in a *laboratory*, but the person in charge of a *laboratory* is not a *technician*. Although choice (A) may seem correct because a MANAGER also works in a STORE, you should realize that an *administrator* also works in a *hospital* (and a *student* works in a *school*). Because only one choice can be correct, you must find a more specific relationship between the capitalized words. When you focus on the supervisory role of a MANAGER, it becomes clear that choice (A) is incorrect.

14. WALLET : MONEY ::

    (A)   safe : lock
    (B)   suitcase : clothing
    (C)   camera : film
    (D)   setting : jewel
    (E)   car : engine

Choice **(B)** is correct. A WALLET is designed primarily for holding and carrying MONEY, just as a *suitcase* is designed primarily for holding and carrying *clothing*.

Choice (C) is incorrect. A *camera* may hold *film* in it, but a camera is designed primarily to take pictures. You would not say that a *camera* is designed primarily for holding and carrying *film*.

15. LUBRICATE : SMOOTHLY ::

    (A)   weigh : heavily
    (B)   assist : grudgingly
    (C)   speak : softly
    (D)   muffle : quietly
    (E)   absorb : quickly

Choice **(D)** is correct. To LUBRICATE is to make something slippery in order to reduce friction. To *muffle* is to wrap or pad something in order to deaden the sound it creates. You would LUBRICATE something to make it move or operate more SMOOTHLY, just as you would *muffle* something to make it move or operate more *quietly*.

Choice (E) is incorrect. To *absorb* is to take something in, either literally (as a sponge *absorbs* water) or metaphorically (as a student *absorbs* information). It is not correct to say that you would *absorb* something to make it move or operate more *quickly*.

16. BIRD : AVIAN ::

 (A) plant : tropical
 (B) meat : carnivorous
 (C) snake : slippery
 (D) dog : canine
 (E) lung : amphibian

Choice **(D)** is correct. Something that is AVIAN is related to or characteristic of a BIRD; for example, an AVIAN enclosure is a BIRD cage. Similarly, something that is *canine* is related to or characteristic of a *dog*; for example, a *canine* restraint is a *dog* leash. Thus, whatever is AVIAN has to do with a BIRD, just as whatever is *canine* has to do with a *dog*.

Choice (A) is incorrect. Something that is *tropical* is related to or characteristic of the Tropics, a geographical zone that lies along the equator. A *plant* might be *tropical*, but so might a bird or a climate. It is incorrect to say that whatever is *tropical* has to do with a *plant*.

17. IRRATIONAL : LOGIC ::

 (A) unrealistic : understanding
 (B) unethical : morality
 (C) illegible : erasure
 (D) infinite : expansion
 (E) factual : verification

Choice **(B)** is correct. Someone who is IRRATIONAL behaves illogically, in a way that defies reason. Similarly, an *unethical* person behaves unscrupulously, in defiance of a conventional moral code. An IRRATIONAL person violates the rules of LOGIC, just as an *unethical* person violates the rules of *morality*.

Choice (A) is incorrect. Someone who is *unrealistic* is unreasonably idealistic. Such a person does not necessarily lack *understanding* altogether but has an *understanding* that is inconsistent with reality. While an *unrealistic* person may defy reality, an *unrealistic* person does not violate the rules of *understanding*.

18. CONSTELLATION : STARS ::

 (A) construction : houses
 (B) honey : bees
 (C) map : boundaries
 (D) train : passengers
 (E) range : mountains

Choice **(E)** is correct. A CONSTELLATION is a formation of individual STARS perceived as a whole. A *range* is a chain of individual *mountains* referred to as a whole. Thus, a CONSTELLATION is a group of STARS, just as a *range* is a group of *mountains*.

Choice (C) is incorrect. A *map* has certain *boundaries* itself, and it may depict various *boundaries* (for example, the *boundaries* between states or nations), but a *map* is not itself a group of *boundaries*.

19. CALCULATOR : COMPUTE ::

(A) plug : insert
(B) clamp : grip
(C) saddle : straddle
(D) bridge : suspend
(E) incinerator : warm

Choice **(B)** is correct. A CALCULATOR is used to perform mathematical computations. A *clamp* is a tool with adjustable sides or parts used for bracing objects or holding them together. A CALCULATOR is a device used to COMPUTE, just as a *clamp* is a device used to *grip*.

Choice **(E)** is incorrect. An *incinerator* is an apparatus, such as a furnace, used to burn up something, unlike a heater, a stove, or a radiator, which are devices used merely to *warm* up something. It is not correct, then, to say that an *incinerator* is a device used to *warm*.

20. EXTRAVAGANT : SPEND ::

(A) belligerent : fight
(B) remarkable : surprise
(C) charitable : receive
(D) antagonistic : agree
(E) persuasive : believe

Choice **(A)** is correct. To be EXTRAVAGANT is to be inclined to make lavish or imprudent expenditures. To be *belligerent* is to be hostile, warlike, or eager to engage in conflicts. A person who is EXTRAVAGANT by definition is likely to SPEND a lot, just as a person who is *belligerent* by definition is likely to *fight* a lot.

Choice **(E)** is incorrect. A person who is *persuasive* is one who can convince others of his or her beliefs, which may be few in number. It is not true that a person who is *persuasive* by definition is likely to *believe* a lot.

21. ARCHITECT : BLUEPRINT ::

(A) instructor : blackboard
(B) graduate : diploma
(C) musician : note
(D) painter : brush
(E) composer : score

Choice **(E)** is correct. A BLUEPRINT is a reproduction of architectural plans or technical drawings for a building or for some other type of structure. A *score* is the written version of a musical composition. A BLUEPRINT is a kind of plan created by an ARCHITECT, just as a *score* is a kind of plan created by a *composer*.

Choice **(C)** is incorrect. A *note* is a musical tone of definite pitch. *Musicians* play *notes* when they perform a musical piece, but it is not true that a *note* is a representation of a complex structure envisioned by a *musician*.

22. WEAVE : FABRIC ::

    (A) illustrate : manual
    (B) hang : picture
    (C) sew : thread
    (D) bake : oven
    (E) write : text

Choice **(E)** is correct. To WEAVE is to make something (like cloth or a basket) by interlacing strands or threads of material—for example on a loom. FABRIC is cloth produced by the knitting or WEAVing of fibers. To WEAVE is to create FABRIC, just as to *write* is to create *text*.

Choice (C) is incorrect. The words *sew* and *thread* are from the same realm as WEAVE and FABRIC, but they do not have the same relationship. To *sew* is to make, repair, or fasten something using a needle and *thread*. It is not true that to *sew* is to create *thread*.

23. TESTIMONY : WITNESS ::

    (A) leadership : follower
    (B) proof : theorist
    (C) expertise : authority
    (D) contradiction : investigator
    (E) confiscation : official

Choice **(C)** is correct. TESTIMONY is a declaration made by a WITNESS under oath, as in a court of law. An *authority* is someone who is especially knowledgeable in a particular field, an accepted source of expert information or advice. A WITNESS by definition is a person who provides TESTIMONY, just as an *authority* by definition is a person who provides *expertise*.

Choice (B) is incorrect. A *theorist* is a person who formulates a theory. *Proof* is the validation of a theory, inductively or deductively, by applying rules or citing evidence. Simply formulating a theory does not require proving it, so it is incorrect to say that a *theorist* by definition is a person who provides *proof*.

24. Passage 1 is best described as a

    (A) tactful response to a controversial question
    (B) personal assessment of a confusing situation
    (C) scathing condemnation of an outdated concept
    (D) general overview of a political institution
    (E) theoretical statement about the value of self-government

Choice **(D)** is correct. The introduction calls the New England town meeting an "institution of local government" because the meeting is an established practice with a long history. The definition of *political* includes the idea of activities involving government. Passage 1 provides a summary or *overview* of the New England town meeting by describing how it originated and how it typically functioned.

Choice (E) is incorrect. The author of Passage 1 makes statements and generalizations based on fact and does not discuss theories or comment on the *value of self-government*. Passage 1 focuses on what the town meeting was, not on whether the town meeting was an example of something valuable.

25. Passage 1 suggests that the most significant innovation of the town meeting was the

   (A) rejection of the parish as being equivalent to the town
   (B) collective decision-making by ordinary citizens
   (C) creation of a local arena for discussion of issues of national interest
   (D) community approval of taxes and expenditures
   (E) definition of "freemen" as a new group in rural society

Choice **(B)** is correct. The question asks which "innovation" or change involving the town meeting is presented in Passage 1 as being the most significant. In the first paragraph of Passage 1, the author refers to "new forms of self-government" and, in line 6, uses "but" to signal that the "comprehensive powers" and "new vitality" of New England town meetings were a significant change from earlier forms of self-government. Lines 8–10 indicate that meetings "came to include all the men who had settled the town" and lines 19–24 indicate the types of decisions made by the town meetings.

Choice (E) is incorrect. Passage 1 does not indicate that "freemen" represented a new group in rural society but instead notes that, in town government, the definition of "freemen" was gradually broadened. "Soon the towns developed their own sort of 'freemen'—a group larger than those whom the General Court of the colony recognized as those granted rights to land" (lines 13–16). Passage 1 presents the changing definition of "freemen" as one of many changes and does not single it out as being more significant than the others.

26. In Passage 1, the author's attitude toward the participants in town meetings is best described as

   (A) admiration of their loyalty to a political ideal
   (B) respect for their active involvement in local government
   (C) sympathy with their frustration with meeting at infrequent intervals
   (D) affection for their naïve trust in purely democratic institutions
   (E) amusement at their willingness to carry petty arguments to local officials

Choice **(B)** is correct. In the second paragraph of Passage 1, the author characterizes town meetings as "debating societies" and then lists a series of facts about participants in town meetings to indicate that they also performed important tasks in a responsible fashion. ("They distributed town lands," "they made crucial decisions about schools, roads, and bridges," and "they elected the selectmen, constables, and others.") Although the author does not directly state an opinion about the participants, the statement "they were more than that" (lines 18–19), followed by the list of facts, expresses the author's respect for the conduct of the participants.

Choice (A) is incorrect. The author of Passage 1 describes the conduct of the participants in ways that signal approval, possibly consistent with *admiration*. However, Passage 1 does not mention the participants' *loyalty to a political ideal* and does not express *admiration* for such loyalty.

27. The author of Passage 1 refers to the Parliamentary Act of 1774 to make the point that town meetings

    (A) **were perceived as fostering political self-determination**
    (B) were regarded as forums for class conflict
    (C) enjoyed prestige only in New England
    (D) had no counterparts in local English government
    (E) represented a long tradition of local self-rule

Choice **(A)** is correct. The last sentence of Passage 1 states that "…as the movement for independence gathered momentum, a British Parliamentary Act of 1774 decreed that no town meeting should be held to discuss affairs of government without written permission from the royal governor." Passage 1 indicates that, as the movement for independence from Britain grew steadily stronger, the British government responded by insisting it approve the town meetings because it perceived the town meetings as fostering or encouraging *political self-determination*.

Choice (D) is incorrect. The beginning of Passage 1 briefly compares forms of local government in Britain and New England in early colonial times, but that comparison is not addressed at all in the final paragraph where the 1774 Act is mentioned. Choice (D) is irrelevant to the question being asked. Remember, when answering reading questions, pay close attention to whether an appealing choice really does answer the question. A choice may seem true or accurate, but still not answer the question.

28. In Passage 2, the author attempts to

    (A) compare two erroneous views
    (B) perpetuate old-fashioned historical beliefs
    (C) explain reasons underlying a poor decision
    (D) **correct a misconception**
    (E) argue for changing a deplorable situation

Choice **(D)** is correct. In lines 48–50 of Passage 2, the author states, "the impression that the town meetings of old were free, democratic, and civilized is far too simplistic." The impression presents a picture of town meetings that is so simple that it is actually inaccurate—*a misconception*. The rest of Passage 2 explains the author's claim and provides information that the author feels is more accurate.

Choice (B) is incorrect. To *perpetuate old-fashioned beliefs* would mean to confirm and support the "New England mythology" that the author of Passage 2 describes in lines 46–50. Instead of confirming and supporting this mythology, the author challenges it as being "too simplistic."

29. In lines 39–45, the author of Passage 2 expresses which of the following for supporters of the myth?

   (A) Scorn
   (B) Impatience
   (C) Dismay
   (D) Admiration
   (E) Sympathy

Choice **(E)** is correct. The author suggests in the beginning of Passage 2 that valuing the idea of the New England town meeting is "entirely understandable" (lines 40–41). Asking "Who can resist the thought that life would be better...?" (lines 42–43) suggests that willingness to believe the myth is an almost inevitable human reaction. The author expresses *sympathy* for the supporters of the myth by identifying with and even defending the way they feel.

Choice (D) is incorrect. In the opening sentence of Passage 2, the author describes the motives of the supporters of the myth as "entirely understandable" (lines 40–41). The author implies that these motives need to be understood and acknowledged, not that the supporters of the myth deserve to be praised or admired.

30. In lines 53–55 ("In . . . selectmen"), the author of Passage 2 distinguishes between the

   (A) general population and a small group
   (B) earliest colonizers and the earliest inhabitants
   (C) rural population and the population of towns
   (D) agricultural labor force and an aristocratic class
   (E) highly educated elite and an illiterate minority

Choice **(A)** is correct. The sentence in lines 53–55 notes that "…it was not 'the people' who ran the town meetings; it was the town selectmen." The author of Passage 2 is pointing out an important difference between two groups of people—the ordinary townsfolk and the selectmen, a much smaller group.

Choice (D) is incorrect. The sentence in lines 53–55 distinguishes between "the people" and the town selectmen, but does not characterize either of these groups as an *agricultural labor force* or an *aristocratic class*.

31. In Passage 2, the author describes the "experiment" (line 63) in a tone that

   (A) objectively summarizes crucial events in a typical town
   (B) enthusiastically reveals a startling discovery
   (C) mildly scolds historians who support inaccurate interpretations
   (D) gently mocks false notions about town meetings
   (E) sharply criticizes the disastrous errors of the first settlers

Choice **(D)** is correct. The author of Passage 2 describes the early experience in Dedham in lines 62–65: "A great and noble experiment, it lasted all of three years." The words "all of three years" underline the inaccuracy of the myth that direct, participatory town meetings endured throughout the entire colonial period in New England. The contrast mocks the myth as a plainly false idea, yet the author presents the idea as representing something "great and noble." The tone criticizes the *false notions* but in a way that is sympathetic rather than hostile.

Choice (B) is incorrect. In Passage 2, the author argues that "the impression that the town meetings of old were free, democratic, and civilized is far too simplistic" (lines 48–50) and supports the generalization with details. The Dedham experience supports the author's argument: the failure indicates that the myth is inaccurate. The author presents the information about Dedham as predictable, not startling, and the tone criticizes the myth.

32. The discussion of Dedham (lines 58–65) serves what function in the development of the argument in Passage 2?

(A) It provides a detailed examination of a case that illustrates an overall pattern.
(B) It refers to an expert to confirm the author's viewpoint.
(C) It gives an example of a fact uncovered only recently by historians.
(D) It compares an atypical, verified example with an inaccurate generalization.
(E) It contrasts a historical incident with a legendary event.

Choice **(D)** is correct. In lines 50–56, the author of Passage 2 challenges the assumption that "at town meetings everybody was allowed to vote." The author argues that this generalization is inaccurate. To demonstrate its inaccuracy further, the author of Passage 2 compares the generalization—"direct, participatory democracy" (lines 61–62)—with the historical case of Dedham, where the policy of allowing townsfolk to vote on all major decisions lasted only three years and so was atypical, different from the usual practices.

Choice (A) is incorrect. Passage 2 does not provide a detailed examination of what happened in Dedham, but instead briefly summarizes the points that are related to the author's argument.

33. Passage 2 suggests that the statement in lines 8–10 ("The New England . . . town") should be qualified by which additional information?

(A) The group was based on a definition set by rural English parishes.
(B) The classification was significantly altered by the British legislation of 1774.
(C) The tradition rejected the claims of female residents of Dedham to full voting rights.
(D) The standard did not recognize property owners as substantial contributors of tax revenues.
(E) The category did not include numerous adults of the community.

Choice **(E)** is correct. What missing information would the author of Passage 2 most likely feel must be added to the sentence to modify it so that it more accurately represents history? While Passage 1 emphasizes that the New England town meetings "came to include all the men who had settled the town" (lines 9–10), Passage 2 emphasizes that they "did not include women, Black people, American Indians, and White men who did not own property" (lines 51–53) as voting members. The author of Passage 2 would feel that the sentence in Passage 1 only tells part of the story and should be qualified by the fact that this *category did not include numerous adults of the community.*

Choice (A) is incorrect. Passage 2 does not discuss the influence of English parishes on the New England town meeting. The author of Passage 2 would not feel the information in choice (A) is relevant to the sentence in lines 8–10 of Passage 1.

34. Which detail discussed in Passage 1 is most consistent with the generalization in lines 72–76 ("When . . . made") ?

(A) The existence of vestry meetings in English parishes
(B) The amenities on which tax revenues were spent
(C) The limit on attendance at town meetings to those designated as freemen
(D) The Massachusetts Bay colony law of 1715
(E) The Parliamentary Act of 1774

Choice **(D)** is correct. The question asks you to decide which detail mentioned in Passage 1 most directly supports the argument made in this part of Passage 2. This part of Passage 2 says, "When meetings were called, it was the selectmen who set the agenda and they who controlled the discussion. Only rarely did townsfolk challenge the decisions the selectmen made." Choice (D) is the only choice that covers issues of the agenda and discussion at town meetings: "A law of 1715 required the selection of moderators, gave them the power to impose fines on those who spoke without permission during meetings, and authorized any ten or more property owners to put items on the agenda" (lines 29–33 in Passage 1). Choice (D), like the quoted part of Passage 2, indicates that a smaller group of people within a town controlled its meetings.

Choice (C) is incorrect. It provides information that is not relevant to the question actually being asked. The limitation on who could attend town meetings does support the overall argument made in Passage 2 that many people were left out of the town meeting process. This question is not asking about the overall argument in Passage 2, but focusing specifically only on lines 72–76 in Passage 2 instead. Remember, reading questions that focus on specific details must have correct answers that address those details. Paying close attention to specific details in the question before you read the five choices may help you rule out the incorrect choices more quickly.

35. Both passages support which generalization about the seventeenth-century town meeting?

(A) Voters were well informed about political issues.
(B) Participants had to have certain qualifications.
(C) Town leaders were frequently replaced after an election.
(D) Meetings discussed matters of national interest.
(E) The most heated debates were about taxes.

Choice **(B)** is correct. Lines 10–13 in Passage 1 indicate that participation in town meetings was at one time limited to "freemen" who met the legal requirements for voting in the colony. Passage 2 indicates that there were "legal property qualifications" (lines 94–95) for voting in town elections and that "suffrage laws" (line 96) put stricter limits on who was entitled to vote.

Choice (D) is incorrect. Although the last sentence of Passage 1 suggests that the British government may have believed town meetings discussed matters and issues that involved events beyond their own towns, Passage 2 does not provide any information about whether town meetings discussed such matters. Choice (D) remains incorrect because it is not supported, as the question requires, by both passages.

36. Which statement best describes a significant difference between the two interpretations of how local taxes were set and collected?

    (A) Passage 1 discusses the burden on taxpayers; Passage 2, the expenses to be met.
    (B) Passage 1 emphasizes details of the process; Passage 2, the results of the process.
    (C) Passage 1 analyzes seventeenth-century patterns; Passage 2, eighteenth-century patterns.
    (D) Each passage presents a different justification for local taxes.
    (E) Each passage identifies a different part of the community as having authority over taxes.

Choice **(E)** is correct. Passage 1 states that the town meetings "levied local taxes" (lines 20–21). Passage 2 differs by stating that the town selectmen "levied the taxes" (lines 55–56). To levy a tax is impose it on the taxpayers and to collect tax payments. The two passages identify two different parts of the community as setting and collecting the taxes.

Choice (B) is incorrect. Neither passage describes the process of setting and collecting taxes. Instead, each passage mentions who held responsibility for the process.

$$x = -2$$
$$y = -x$$

1.

$4x^2$	$8y$

Choice **(C)** is correct. If $x = -2$, then $y = -(-2) = 2$. In Column A, $4x^2 = 4(-2)^2 = 4 \times 4 = 16$ and in Column B, $8y = 8 \times 2 = 16$. Therefore, the values of the quantities in Columns A and B are equal.

Points P and Q lie on line ℓ.
Point R does not lie on line ℓ.

2.

The length of PQ	The length of PR

Choice **(D)** is correct.

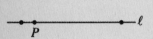

Looking at the figure above, if the point to the left of P is point Q, then PQ is shorter than PR. If, however, the point to the right of P is point Q, then PQ is longer than PR. So there is no way of knowing which segment is longer.

A bracelet that costs a merchant $24 is sold to a
customer at 10 percent above the merchant's cost.

3.

The price the customer paid for the bracelet	$26

Choice **(A)** is correct. The customer paid 10 percent more than the $24 that the merchant paid, or $2.40 more. Therefore, the customer paid $26.40.

The ratio of n to 9 is equal to the ratio of 151 to 197.

4.

n	9

Choice **(B)** is correct. The ratio $\dfrac{151}{197}$ is less than 1, so $\dfrac{n}{9}$ is also less than 1. This means that n must be less than 9, and the quantity in Column B is greater than the quantity in Column A.

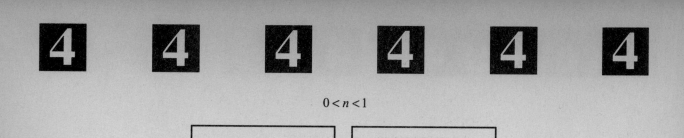

$$0 < n < 1$$

5.

| $(6.5 + n)$ rounded to the nearest whole number | 7 |

Choice **(C)** is correct. In rounding to the nearest whole number, round the number up if the digit in the tenths place of a decimal numeral is 5 or greater. Round the number down if the number in the tenths place is 4 or less. Since $0 < n < 1$, adding n to 6.5 will result in a number that is strictly between 6.5 and 7.5. Any number in that range rounds to 7, so the numbers in both Column A and Column B are equal.

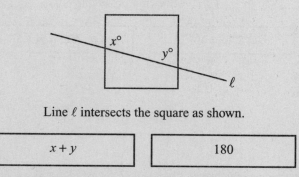

Line ℓ intersects the square as shown.

6.

| $x + y$ | 180 |

Choice **(C)** is correct. Since the four-sided figure is a square, its opposite sides are parallel to each other. Line ℓ is a transversal that intersects one pair of opposite sides. The angles with measures $x°$ and $y°$ are interior angles on the same side of the transversal, so their degree measures add up to 180. Another way to approach this problem is to notice that the angles whose measures are $x°$ and $y°$ belong to a quadrilateral formed by the transversal and the upper part of the square. If you know that the sum of the measures of the angles in a quadrilateral is 360°, you know that $x + y + 90 + 90 = 360$. It follows that $x + y = 180$.

A flat coin is $0.1d$ inches thick.

7.

| The height of a stack of 25 of these coins | $0.25d$ inches |

Choice **(A)** is correct. Since each coin is $0.1d$ inches thick, the height of a stack of 25 of these coins is $25(0.1d)$ inches. 25 times 0.1 is 2.5, so the stack is $2.5d$ inches high. $2.5d > 0.25d$, so the quantity in Column A is greater than the quantity in Column B.

Choice (C) is incorrect. You must be careful when multiplying with decimal points. Multiplying 25×0.1 incorrectly might give you the incorrect result of 0.25.

c is the circumference of a circle with radius r and diameter d. $(r > 0)$

8.

| $\dfrac{c}{d}$ | $\dfrac{c}{r}$ |

Choice **(B)** is correct. Since $r > 0$, c and d will both be positive as well. The fractions in both boxes have the same numerators, so it is only necessary to compare the denominators of the fractions. The diameter of a circle is twice the radius; that is, $d = 2r$. Since $\dfrac{c}{r}$ has a smaller denominator than $\dfrac{c}{d}$, it follows that $\dfrac{c}{r} > \dfrac{c}{d}$.

9.

| 5 added to x | x subtracted from 5 |

Choice **(D)** is correct. Columns A and B can be written as $5 + x$ and $5 - x$, respectively. Notice that both quantities include 5. If 5 is subtracted from both quantities, the comparison is between x and $-x$. Since there is no indication whether x is positive or negative, it is impossible to determine whether x or $-x$ is greater.

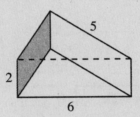

The surface of the solid shown consists of two identical triangular faces and three different rectangular faces. The area of each triangular face is 9.

10.

| The perimeter of the shaded rectangular face | 6 |

Choice **(A)** is correct. Each triangular face has sides of length 5, 6, and x, where x is also the length of a side of the shaded face. By the triangle inequality, you know $5 + x > 6$, so that $x > 1$. The perimeter of the shaded face is

$$2(2) + 2(x) = 4 + 2x > 4 + 2 = 6.$$

11.

The number of different numbers that can be formed by rearranging the digits in the number 2,024, keeping 2 in the thousands place	The number of different numbers that can be formed by rearranging the digits in the number 2,224, keeping 2 in the thousands place

Choice **(A)** is correct. "Keeping 2 in the thousands place" means you want to look at numbers of the form 2, _ _ _ , where the blanks can be filled with the digits 0, 2, and 4 in any order for Column A, or 2, 2, and 4 in Column B. Since the two 2s in Column B are indistinguishable, there are more ways to arrange the digits in Column A. A list of the possibilities will verify this.

Column A	Column B
2,024	2,224
2,042	2,242
2,204	2,422
2,240	
2,402	
2,420	

$$2x + y = 26$$
x and y are integers.
$$y < 0$$

12.

The greatest possible value of y	-1

Choice **(B)** is correct. First, solve the equation above for y.

$$2x + y = 26$$
$$y = 26 - 2x$$

You are told that x and y are each integers and that y is less than 0. In the equation, for y to be less than 0, x has to be greater than 13. The next integer after 13 is 14. When x is 14,

$$y = 26 - 2(14)$$
$$y = 26 - 28$$
$$y = -2$$

The greatest possible value of y is -2, since greater values of x will make y smaller. Therefore, the values $y = -2$ and $x = 14$ satisfy the two requirements that x and y be integers and that y be less than 0. Since $-1 > -2$, the answer is B.

$$X = \{1,3,5,7\}$$
$$Y = \{2,4,6,8\}$$

Sixteen pairs of numbers will be formed by pairing each member of X with each member of Y. A pair will be chosen at random.

13.

The probability that the sum of the pair of numbers will be even	The probability that the sum of the pair of numbers will be odd

Choice **(B)** is correct. Notice that the members of set X are odd integers, while the members of set Y are even integers. Each of the sixteen pairs of numbers formed will consist of exactly one odd number (from set X) and exactly one even number (from set Y). The sum of the two numbers in each of these 16 pairs will necessarily be odd because the sum of an even integer and an odd integer is always an odd integer. Therefore, the probability in Column A is $\frac{0}{16} = 0$ and the probability in Column B is $\frac{16}{16} = 1$. The quantity in Column B is greater than the quantity in Column A.

$$a > 1$$
$$\frac{a^{16}}{a^x} = \frac{a^x}{a^4}$$

14.

x	8

Choice **(A)** is correct. The inequality $a > 1$ tells you that you can rule out the case of $a = 0$ and $a = 1$. The equation can be rewritten as $(a^x)(a^x) = (a^{16})(a^4)$, which can be simplified to $a^{2x} = a^{20}$. This means that $2x = 20$, since the base of each of the expressions is a. Hence, $x = 10$, which is greater than 8.

The sum of the ages of Juanita's sisters is equal to the sum of the ages of her brothers.

15.

The sum of the ages of Juanita's sisters 5 years from now	The sum of the ages of Juanita's brothers 6 years from now

Choice **(D)** is correct. In this question, it is important that the <u>number</u> of Juanita's sisters and the <u>number</u> of Juanita's brothers is not given. Let m equal the sum of the ages of her sisters, which is also equal to the sum of the ages of her brothers. If Juanita has 3 sisters and 2 brothers, then 5 years from now the sum of the ages of her sisters will be $m + (3 \times 5) = m + 15$, and 6 years from now the sum of the ages of her brothers will be $m + (2 \times 6) = m + 12$. In this case the quantity in Column A is greater than the quantity in Column B. If, on the other hand, she has 2 sisters and 3 brothers, $m + (2 \times 5) = m + 10$, which is less than $m + (3 \times 6) = m + 18$. In this case, the quantity in Column B is greater than the quantity in Column A. The relationship cannot be determined because there is not enough information, namely the numbers of Juanita's brothers and sisters.

16. If $x = 16$ is a solution to the equation $9x - k = 130$, where k is a constant, what is the value of k?

The correct answer is **14**. To find the value of k, substitute 16 into the equation for x: $9(16) - k = 130$ or $k = 144 - 130 = 14$.

17. If $xy = 10$, $yz = 30$, and $y^2 = \dfrac{1}{9}$, what is the value of xz?

The correct answer is **2700**. One way to solve this problem is to solve the first equation for x and the second equation for z. $x = \dfrac{10}{y}$ and $z = \dfrac{30}{y}$. Then the product $xz = \dfrac{10}{y} \cdot \dfrac{30}{y} = \dfrac{300}{y^2}$. Since you need a value for xz, substitute $\dfrac{1}{9}$ in the expression for y^2, which results in $xz = \dfrac{300}{\frac{1}{9}} = 300 \times 9 = 2700$. Another approach is to multiply the quantities in the first two equations that are given in the question to get $xy^2z = 300$. Then substitute $\dfrac{1}{9}$ for y^2 to get $\dfrac{1}{9}xz = 300$. Multiply both sides of this equation by 9 to get $xz = 2700$.

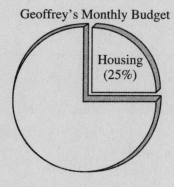

Geoffrey's Monthly Budget

Housing (25%)

18. On the basis of the information in the graph above, if Geoffrey's monthly housing budget is $650, what is the dollar amount of his total monthly budget? (Disregard the $ sign when gridding your answer.)

The correct answer is **2600**. The graph indicates that 25% or one-fourth of the total budget is spent on housing. If $650 is one-fourth of the budget, multiply by 4 to find the total budget: $4 \times \$650 = \$2600$.

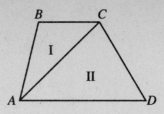

19. In the figure above, the area of triangle I is $\frac{1}{2}$ the area of triangle II. If $BC \parallel AD$ and the sum of the lengths of BC and AD is 18, what is the length of AD ?

The correct answer is **12**. Since $BC \parallel AD$, both triangles have the same height, as shown in the figure below.

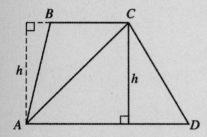

The sum of the lengths BC and AD is 18. If x represents the length of AD, then $18 - x$ represents the length of BC, as shown below.

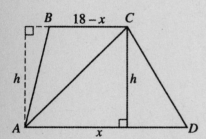

The area of a triangle is given by the formula $A = \frac{1}{2}hb$, where b is the base of the triangle and h is its height or altitude. Any side of the triangle can be considered the base, but the altitude must be drawn perpendicular to that side. The area of

$\triangle ABC = \frac{1}{2}h(18 - x)$ and the area of $\triangle ACD = \frac{1}{2}hx$. Since the area of $\triangle ACD$ is twice the area of

$\triangle ABC$, $\frac{1}{2}hx = 2\left(\frac{1}{2}\right)h(18 - x) = h(18 - x)$. Solve the equation $\frac{1}{2}hx = h(18 - x)$ for x.

$hx = 2h(18 - x)$

$x = 36 - 2x$

$3x = 36$

$x = 12$, the length of AD.

20. What is one possible value of x for which $x < 2 < \frac{1}{x}$?

The correct answer is any number x such that $\mathbf{0 < x < \frac{1}{2}}$. You are given $x < 2 < \frac{1}{x}$, which means that x is less than 2 and $\frac{1}{x}$ is greater than 2. x must be greater than 0, otherwise $\frac{1}{x}$ would be undefined or negative, but you already know that it is greater than 2. Solving the inequality $2 < \frac{1}{x}$, $2x < 1$ and $x < \frac{1}{2}$. Hence, x must be both greater than 0 and less than $\frac{1}{2}$. For example, x could be $\frac{1}{4}, \frac{1}{3}, \frac{2}{5}$, etc. Choose any one of these, such as $x = \frac{2}{5}$, to check your answer by seeing that the given inequalities are satisfied: $\frac{2}{5} < 2 < \frac{5}{2}$.

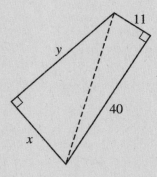

21. In the figure above, what is the value of $x^2 + y^2$?

The correct answer is **1721**. The diagonal of the quadrilateral (the dashed line segment in the figure) separates the region into two right triangles. If d represents the length of the diagonal, the Pythagorean Theorem can then be applied to each of the two right triangles: $x^2 + y^2 = d^2 = 11^2 + 40^2$. So $x^2 + y^2 = 11^2 + 40^2 = 121 + 1600 = 1721$.

22. For all numbers x and y, where $x \neq y$, let $x \blacktriangle y$ be defined as $\dfrac{x+y}{x-y}$. If $8 \blacktriangle w = \dfrac{4}{3}$, what is the value of w?

The correct answer is **8/7** or **1.14**. You are given $x \blacktriangle y = \dfrac{x+y}{x-y}$ and $8 \blacktriangle w = \dfrac{4}{3}$. Therefore, $8 \blacktriangle w = \dfrac{8+w}{8-w} = \dfrac{4}{3}$. In a proportion such as this, the product of the means, 4 and $8-w$, equals the product of the extremes, 3 and $8+w$.

That is, $3(8+w) = 4(8-w)$

$$24 + 3w = 32 - 4w$$
$$7w = 8$$
$$w = \frac{8}{7} \text{ or } 1.14$$

23. Roberta rode her bicycle a total of 169 miles in 13 days. Each day after the first day she rode 1 mile farther than the day before. What was the difference between the average (arithmetic mean) number of miles she rode per day and the median number of miles she rode during the 13 days?

The correct answer is **0**. The average (arithmetic mean) of a set of numbers is determined by finding the sum of the numbers and then dividing by how many numbers there are. To find the average number of miles Roberta rode each day, divide the total mileage by the number of days. The sum is given as 169, so 169 miles divided by 13 days is 13 miles per day.

Since Roberta rode 1 mile farther each day than she did the day before, the number of miles increased in order over the 13 days. The median number of miles she rode over the 13 days is the number of miles that she rode on the middle day, which is the 7th day. Suppose she rode x miles on the first day. She rode $x+1$ miles on the second day, $x+2$ miles on the third day, and so forth until the thirteenth day, on which she rode $x+12$ miles. The total number of miles she rode is $13x + 1 + 2 + \ldots + 12$ miles, which is $13x + 78$ miles. Remember that this total equals 169. Solve the equation

$$13x + 78 = 169$$
$$13x = 91$$
$$x = 7$$

If $x = 7$, and Roberta rode $x + 6$ miles on the 7th day, the median number of miles she rode during the 13 days was 13. Since the median number of miles and the average number of miles are each 13, their difference is 0.

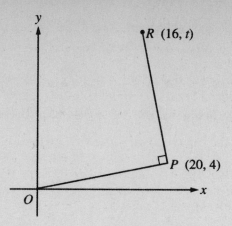

24. In the *xy*-plane above, $OP = PR$. What is the value of t ?

The correct answer is **24**. One way to solve this is to use the Pythagorean Theorem or distance formula.

If two points have coordinates (x_1, y_1) and (x_2, y_2), respectively, then the distance beween them is $\sqrt{(x_2 - x_1)^2 + (y_2 - y_1)^2}$.

Using the points (0, 0) and (20, 4), the length of OP is $\sqrt{20^2 + 4^2}$ or $\sqrt{416}$.

Using the points (16, *t*) and (20, 4), the length of PR is $\sqrt{(20 - 16)^2 + (4 - t)^2}$. Therefore,

$\sqrt{416} = \sqrt{(20 - 16)^2 + (4 - t)^2}$. Square both sides of the equation to get

$$416 = (20 - 16)^2 + (4 - t)^2$$
$$416 = 16 + (4 - t)^2$$
$$400 = (4 - t)^2$$

Therefore, $4 - t = 20$ or $4 - t = -20$, and it follows that $t = -16$ or $t = 24$. Since R is in the first quadrant, t is positive; hence, t equals 24.

25. A flock of geese on a pond were being observed continuously. At 1:00 P.M., $\frac{1}{5}$ of the geese flew away. At 2:00 P.M., $\frac{1}{8}$ of the geese that remained flew away. At 3:00 P.M., 3 times as many geese as had flown away at 1:00 P.M. flew away, leaving 28 geese on the pond. At no other times did any geese arrive or fly away. How many geese were in the original flock?

The correct answer is **280**. Solve this problem by translating the information into algebraic equations. First, let *g* stand for

the number of geese in the original flock. At 1:00, $\frac{g}{5}$ flew away, leaving $\frac{4}{5}g$. At 2:00, $\frac{1}{8}$ of the remaining geese, or

$\frac{1}{8}\left(\frac{4}{5}g\right)$, or $\frac{1}{10}g$, flew away. Now $\frac{4}{5}g - \frac{1}{10}g = \frac{7}{10}g$ geese remained. At 3:00, 3 times the number that had flown away

at 1:00, or $\frac{3}{5}g$, flew away. So $\frac{7}{10}g - \frac{3}{5}g$, or $\frac{1}{10}g$ geese are left. If $\frac{1}{10}g = 28$, then $g = 280$.

1. The exercise involving the desktop globe (lines 8–10) is meant to

    (A) suggest that a determined student can master the complexities of ecology
    (B) compare the diversity of life on different continents
    (C) reiterate the comparatively small size of Earth
    (D) emphasize that most of life on Earth is invisible to the naked eye
    (E) illustrate the extent of the biosphere relative to the size of Earth

Choice **(E)** is correct. In lines 3–5, the author indicates that the biosphere "makes up only about one part in ten billion of Earth's mass." To help the reader visualize how tiny a fraction this is, the author asks the reader in lines 8–10 to imagine how things would look if Earth were scaled down to the size of a desktop globe and its surface were viewed edgewise at arm's length. In contrast to Earth, which would be large enough to be easily visible, the biosphere would be so thin that it could not be seen with the naked eye. This illustrates the small *extent of the biosphere relative to the size of Earth*.

Choice (D) is incorrect. The author notes in lines 8–10 that the biosphere would be invisible to the naked eye if "the world were the size of an ordinary desktop globe." This is an observation about a hypothetical circumstance. The author does not consider the issue of whether or not most of Earth's life forms are *invisible to the naked eye*.

2. The reference to "ten seconds" in line 24 primarily serves to

    (A) show the consequences of a single action
    (B) suggest the brief life spans of many species
    (C) illustrate the space occupied by most life
    (D) demonstrate the invulnerability of life on Earth
    (E) indicate the frustration of snatching brief insights

Choice **(C)** is correct. In the second paragraph the author uses the illustration of taking a walk from the center of Earth to a point a few miles above Earth's surface, a process said to take a little over 12 weeks. The time it takes to go through the part of the biosphere where most of life can be found is a mere ten seconds. This illustrates the relatively tiny *space occupied by most life*—a space covered in just ten seconds during a journey that lasts over 12 weeks.

Choice (B) is incorrect. There is no reference in the second paragraph to the lifespan of any species.

3. In line 29, the author mentions "airliners" to illustrate that

    (A) natural biorhythms are routinely disrupted
    (B) life on Earth is mostly limited to the surface
    (C) humans are the most mobile species
    (D) intelligence affects the survival of a species
    (E) life-forms just above the surface of Earth are diverse

Choice **(B)** is correct. In the second paragraph the author indicates that there is a "dazzling burst of life" featuring "tens of thousands of species" at Earth's surface (lines 23–26), but that "almost all" of this life is gone at a half-minute's walking distance above Earth (line 27), and "only the faintest traces" of life remain at a height of several miles, "consisting largely of people in airliners who are filled in turn with bacteria" (lines 28–30). The author mentions "airliners" in the course of showing that there is far more life on Earth's surface than anywhere else in the biosphere.

Choice (A) is incorrect. The mention of airliners in line 29 has nothing to do with the disruption of natural biorhythms, an issue that is not even implicitly raised in the passage.

4. The author argues that the central aspect of the "hallmark of life" (line 31) is essentially

    (A) competition for energy
    (B) competition for sunlight
    (C) competition for space
    (D) efficient use of energy
    (E) an incessant flow of energy

Choice **(A)** is correct. In lines 31–33 the author defines the "hallmark of life" as "a struggle among…organisms…for a vanishingly small amount of energy." Choice (A), *competition for energy*, best captures this notion.

Choice (D) is incorrect. The author's definition of the hallmark of life focuses on the competition for energy among organisms, not on the *efficient use of energy*.

5. In line 37, "discounted" most nearly means

    (A) devalued
    (B) disregarded
    (C) discredited
    (D) reduced
    (E) underestimated

Choice **(D)** is correct. Lines 38–46 describe in detail how energy is "discounted" as it passes through the levels of the food web. Plants capture 10 percent of the Sun's energy; 10 percent of that energy passes to the organisms that eat plants; 10 percent of that passes to the next level, and so on until the top level is reached. The meaning of "discounted" that best fits this context is *reduced*, as a very small portion of the Sun's energy that reaches Earth is captured by the top level of the food web.

Choice (B) is incorrect. The process described in lines 38–46 results in the decrease or reduction of energy as it passes from the lowest levels of the food web to the highest. Energy is not *disregarded* or neglected, it is *reduced*.

6. In line 48, the author uses "predestined" to convey the

    (A) unavoidable influence of change in the natural world
    (B) intensity of the instincts of carnivores
    (C) inevitability of the size and number of certain organisms
    (D) outcome of predictable conflicts between animals of different sizes
    (E) consistency of behavior across species

Choice **(C)** is correct. The word "predestined" means determined beforehand, fated. The author says that the top carnivores "are predestined…to be big in size and sparse in number" (lines 47–49). In other words, the *size and number of certain organisms* (the top carnivores) is inevitable.

Choice (D) is incorrect. Lines 46–49 state that the position of certain carnivores at the top of the food web predestines, or predetermines, their size and number. There is no mention of conflicts between animals of different sizes.

7. The passage indicates that which group receives the smallest amount of energy?

    (A) Green plants
    (B) Herbivores
    (C) Low- and middle-level carnivores
    (D) Top-level carnivores
    (E) Bacteria

Choice **(D)** is correct. The third paragraph describes the process by which the Sun's energy that reaches Earth passes through the lowest levels of the food web to the highest, which is occupied by the top carnivores. As the energy passes upward, most of it is lost. The *top-level carnivores* "live on such a small portion of life's available energy as always to skirt the edge of extinction" (lines 50–51).

Choice (A) is incorrect. Plants occupy the lowest level of the food web, and are eaten by "caterpillars and other herbivores" (lines 39–40). Since energy is sharply reduced as it passes from the lowest to the highest level, plants would receive the greatest amount of energy, not the smallest.

8. The two pyramids described in the passage are similar in which of the following ways?

    I. Green plants are at the bottom.
    II. Decomposers are at the second level.
    III. Large carnivores are at the top.

    (A) I only
    (B) III only
    (C) I and II only
    (D) I and III only
    (E) I, II, and III

Choice **(D)** is correct. The last two paragraphs describe the energy pyramid and the biomass pyramid. According to the passage, in both pyramids the lowest level is occupied by plants while the highest is occupied by the big carnivores.

Choice (B) is incorrect. While it is true that in both the energy pyramid and the biomass pyramid *large carnivores are at the top* level, this choice is only partially accurate, as it does not take into account green plants, which are said to occupy the same relative level in each pyramid: the bottom.

9. In lines 75–76, "No one looks twice" emphasizes that certain animal species are

    (A) unappealing
    (B) short-lived
    (C) timid
    (D) small
    (E) plentiful

Choice **(E)** is correct. Lines 75–78 state that "No one looks twice at a sparrow or a squirrel...but glimpsing a peregrine falcon or a mountain lion is a lifetime experience." The falcon and the mountain lion are top carnivores, which are said to be "so scarce that the very sight of one in the wild is memorable" (lines 74–75). The implication is that no one looks twice at a sparrow or a squirrel because species such as sparrows and squirrels are *plentiful* and commonplace.

Choice (A) is incorrect. What makes species such as sparrows and squirrels unworthy of a second look is not their lack of appeal but, rather, the fact that there are so many of them around.

10. Which animal would be the most appropriate example to add to the two special animals mentioned in lines 77–78?

    (A) Racehorse
    (B) Grizzly bear
    (C) Garden snake
    (D) Pigeon
    (E) Rat

Choice **(B)** is correct. Lines 77–78 refer to a peregrine falcon and a mountain lion, top carnivores so rare that seeing one is a lifetime experience. Among the animals named in choices (A) to (E), only the *grizzly bear* is a top carnivore likely to provide one who glimpses it with the experience of a lifetime.

Choice (D) is incorrect. Although, like the falcon, a *pigeon* is a creature of flight, it is common, like the sparrow, and not worthy of special notice.

11. The author assumes that a house cat (line 80) is

    (A) aggressive
    (B) pampered
    (C) playful
    (D) interesting
    (E) endangered

Choice **(A)** is correct. Lines 77–80 state that a glimpse of a peregrine falcon or a mountain lion is memorable "not just because of their size (think of a cow) or ferocity (think of a house cat)." The implication is that, just as a cow, though large, is unexciting, so is a house cat, though potentially ferocious, or aggressively violent, ultimately unremarkable.

Choice (C) is incorrect. Though a house cat can be *playful*, the author is making the point that a house cat, though fierce, is commonplace.

12. The tone of the passage is primarily one of

    (A) detached inquiry
    (B) playful skepticism
    (C) mild defensiveness
    (D) informed appreciation
    (E) urgent entreaty

Choice **(D)** is correct. The author provides enough factual background to achieve an informed tone. With references to the "most wonderful mystery of life" (line 1), the "dazzling burst of life" (line 24), the "immense variety of organisms" (line 32), and the "lifetime experience" (line 78) that glimpsing a peregrine falcon or a mountain lion provides, the author expresses an appreciation of life's richness and multiplicity.

Choice (C) is incorrect. Nowhere does the author show any concern that the views expressed in the passage might be challenged or criticized.

1. If $x + 2y = 8$ and $4y = 4$, what is the value of x ?

   (A) 0
   (B) 2
   (C) 4
   (D) 6
   (E) 7

Choice **(D)** is correct. If $4y = 4$, then $y = 1$, and $2y = 2$. Substituting 2 for $2y$ in the other equation gives $x + 2 = 8$ and $x = 6$.

2. What is the least positive integer that is a multiple of 4, 15, and 18 ?

   (A)   30
   (B)   60
   (C)   180
   (D)   360
   (E) 1,080

Choice **(C)** is correct. Express each of the integers as a product of primes.

$$4 = 2^2$$
$$15 = 3 \times 5$$
$$18 = 2 \times 3^2$$

The least common multiple of the three numbers is the smallest number composed of all the prime factors of each of the three numbers. That is, $2^2 \times 3^2 \times 5 = 180$. Do not include fewer prime factors than is necessary, such as in choice (B), $60 = 2^2 \times 3 \times 5$, which does not include enough factors of 3. Hence, 60 is not a multiple of 18. Similarly, do not include more prime factors than is necessary, as in choice (D), $360 = 2^3 \times 3^2 \times 5$, which includes three factors of 2. Although 360 is a common multiple of the three numbers, it is not the <u>least</u> common multiple.

3. Which of the following is an expression for 10 less than the product of x and 2 ?

   (A) $x^2 - 10$

   (B) $2(x - 10)$

   (C) $(x + 2) - 10$

   (D) $10 - 2x$

   (E) $2x - 10$

Choice **(E)** is correct. Since the product of 2 and x can be represented by $2x$, it follows that 10 less than the product can be represented by $2x - 10$. It may be instructive to notice what some of the other options represent. Choice (A) represents 10 less than the square of x, while choice (D) represents $2x$ less than 10. Choice (C) represents 10 less than the <u>sum</u> of x and 2, and choice (B) represents the product of 2 and the quantity that is 10 less than x.

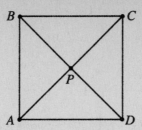

4. The figure above shows a square and five labeled points. What is the least number of these five points that need to be moved so that all five points lie on the same circle?

   (A) **One**
   (B) Two
   (C) Three
   (D) Four
   (E) Five

Choice **(A)** is correct. No circle can pass through all five points. Since the diagonals of a square are equal in length and bisect each other, there is exactly one circle that contains points A, B, C, and D. The center of this circle is P. If the point P were moved to a point on this circle, the five points would all lie on the same circle.

5. How many <u>minutes</u> are required for a car to go 10 miles at a constant speed of 60 miles per hour?

   (A) 600
   (B) 100
   (C) 60
   (D) **10**
   (E)   6

Choice **(D)** is correct. Use the fact that distance equals rate times time for constant speeds.

$$d = r \times t \quad \text{or} \quad 10 \text{ miles} = \frac{60 \text{ miles}}{\text{hour}} \times t$$

Solving for t, $t = \dfrac{10 \text{ miles}}{\left(60\dfrac{\text{miles}}{\text{hour}}\right)} = \dfrac{1}{6} \text{ hour.}$

Converting to minutes, $t = \dfrac{1}{6} \text{ hour} \times \dfrac{60 \text{ minutes}}{\text{hour}} = 10 \text{ minutes.}$

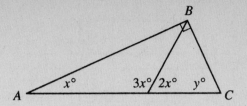

Note: Figure not drawn to scale.

6. In right triangle ABC above, what is the value of y ?

 (A) 45
 (B) 48
 (C) 54
 (D) 60
 (E) 72

Choice **(C)** is correct. Since $\triangle ABC$ is a right triangle, it follows that $x + y + 90 = 180$ or $x + y = 90$. You can determine the value of y if you know the value of x. Notice that there is some additional information in the figure about x, namely that $3x + 2x = 180$ or $5x = 180$, so $x = 36$. Hence, $36 + y = 90$ and $y = 54$.

Questions 7-8 refer to the following information.

1	2	3

4	5	6

The diagram above represents six building lots along a street. There are no other residential sites in the area. Five families—$v, w, x, y,$ and z—are each interested in purchasing a lot, with the following restrictions.

v will occupy lot 6.
y and z will live on different sides of the street.
w and x will live on the same side of the street, and
x will be the only next-door neighbor that w has.
One lot will remain unsold.

7. If all five families purchased lots and fulfilled all the restrictions, which of the following pairs of lots could be the ones purchased by y and z ?

(A) 1 and 2
(B) 1 and 3
(C) 2 and 3
(D) 3 and 5
(E) 3 and 6

Choice **(D)** is correct. One of the restrictions listed for y and z is that they live on different sides of the street. Therefore, choices (A), (B), and (C) can be eliminated since these three pairs involve lots on the same side of the street. Choice (E) can be eliminated since v occupies lot 6. Choice (D) is the only answer choice that contains lots that <u>could</u> be purchased by y and z.

8. If all five families purchased lots and fulfilled all the restrictions and if y purchased lot 3, which of the following must be true?

    I. w purchased lot 1.
    II. x purchased lot 4.
   III. z purchased lot 5.

(A) I only
(B) II only
(C) III only
(D) I and III
(E) II and III

Choice **(A)** is correct. It is given that v will occupy lot 6 and that y will purchase lot 3. Since y and z will live on different sides of the street, one of them must be on the same side with v. There is only one lot unaccounted for on that side of the street. Since w and x will live on the same side of the street, it is not possible for w and x to live on the same side of the street as v. Therefore, w and x will purchase lots 1 and 2 and, furthermore, w will purchase lot 1, since it only has one neighbor.

    I. w purchased lot 1 is a true statement.
    II. x cannot purchase lot 4 since it is on the wrong side of the street.
   III. z could purchase either lot 4 or lot 5.

Only I must be true, so the correct answer is choice (A).

9. In a plane, lines are drawn through a given point O so that the measure of <u>each</u> nonoverlapping angle formed about point O is $60°$. How many different lines are there?

(A) Two
(B) Three
(C) Four
(D) Five
(E) Six

Choice **(B)** is correct. The following figure shows three lines intersecting at point O, forming six angles of $60°$ each.

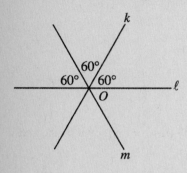

10. For how many different positive integer values of k does $(kx - 6)^2 = 0$ have integer solutions?

(A) None
(B) One
(C) Two
(D) Four
(E) Six

Choice **(D)** is correct. There is only one number whose square is zero, and that number is zero. So $kx - 6 = 0$ or $kx = 6$. In order for k to be a positive integer and for the solutions to be integers, k and x must both be positive integers whose product is 6. There are four pairs of values, k and x, that satisfy this condition: $k = 1$ and $x = 6$, $k = 2$ and $x = 3$, $k = 3$ and $x = 2$, and $k = 6$ and $x = 1$. In particular there are **four** values of k that satisfy the conditions of the question.

It is often the case that a quadratic equation has two solutions, where two possible values of x make the equation true. But for this equation, there are two unknowns, k and x, and the question asks for the number of different positive integer values of k for which x will be an integer. This is a bit different than finding a solution to the usual quadratic equation.